lonely 🌐

New England &
the Mid-Atlantic's

NATIONAL PARKS

Contents

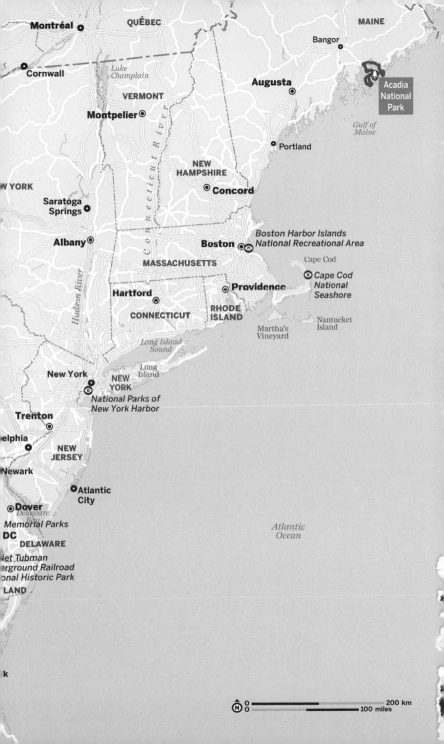

Welcome to New England & the Mid-Atlantic's National Parks

The national parks of New England and the Mid-Atlantic encompass age-old mountains, biologically diverse forests and rugged coastlines formed during the last ice age. Come for scenic drives or multi-month adventures, as well as eye-opening visits to America's most important historic sites.

It's just after sunrise and a few lone hikers scramble up the rocky summit high above the forested slopes. In the morning light, undulating Appalachian peaks glow in subtle shades of blue and violet as they stretch seemingly without end toward the horizon. Elsewhere travelers are rafting through steep-walled gorges, cycling old carriage roads and rock-climbing up sea cliffs as the waves crash against the craggy shore.

The national parks here offer countless adventures and opportunities to connect with nature. You can stroll glacier-carved shores while breathing in the salt-tinged air, or watch cloudless skies over wetlands fill with birds during the fall migration. There's wading into waterfall-filled streams in search of salamanders, stumbling upon white-tailed deer ambling across a sun-kissed meadow, and the simple pleasures of sitting by the campfire and watching the sky fill up with stars.

History is also woven into these protected landscapes. The highs and lows of the country's complicated past are preserved amid the memorials, torch-bearing monuments and battlefields that you'll find in this captivating corner.

> *The national parks here offer countless adventures*

Bass Harbor Head Lighthouse

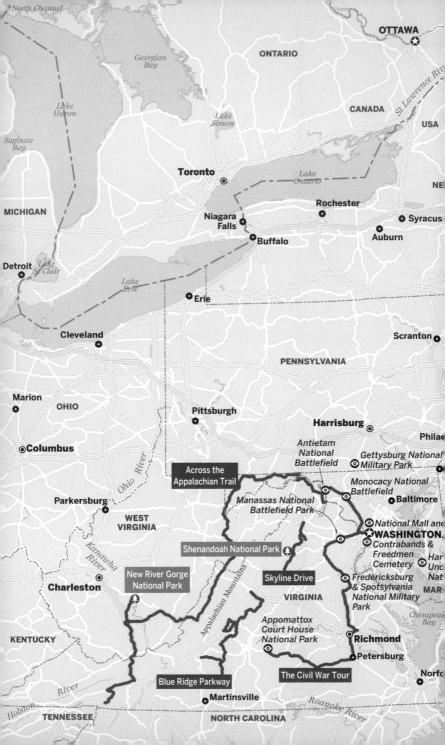

COVID-19

We have re-checked every business in this book before publication to ensure that it is still open after the COVID-19 outbreak. However, the economic and social impacts of COVID-19 will continue to be felt long after the outbreak has been contained, and many businesses, services and events referenced in this guide may experience ongoing restrictions. Some businesses may be temporarily closed, have changed their opening hours and services, or require bookings; some unfortunately could have closed permanently. We suggest you check with venues before visiting for the latest information.

Left: Shenandoah National Park; Above: New River Gorge National Park

Plan Your Trip

New England & the Mid-Atlantic's National Parks Top 9

Acadia National Park

The mountains meet the sea

Miles of rocky coastline and even more miles of hiking and biking trails make this wonderland (p38) Maine's most popular destination – and deservedly so. The high point (literally) is Cadillac Mountain, a 1530ft peak where early risers can catch the country's first sunrise. Later in the day, cool off with a dip in Echo Lake, enjoy some downtime on Sand Beach or linger over tea and popovers near Jordan Pond.

Shenandoah National Park

Forest-covered mountains line the horizon

The view of rolling mountains and the lush Shenandoah Valley will take your breath away at the Hawksbill Mountain summit. We mean that literally; at 4050ft, it's the highest peak in the park (p62). You have to hike to get there, but the 360-degree panorama is worth it. Overlooks, trails and campgrounds hug the Skyline Drive (p66), a 105-mile byway that traverses the whole park. As for wildlife, there's plenty; you're almost guaranteed to see a white-tailed deer.

Appalachian Trail

America's most famous long-distance trek

The country's longest footpath (p92) stretches more than 2100 miles, crosses six national parks and slices through 14 states from Georgia to Maine. Deep woods, craggy peaks, cow-dotted farms and foraging bears are part of the landscape. You needn't conquer the whole thing to experience the magic, though. You can walk portions of it or explore the mountains and forests surrounding the trail on a road trip.

3

Blue Ridge Parkway

A scenic road trip over the mountains

There's not one stoplight to spoil the ride on this 469-mile roadway (p98) traversing the southern Appalachian Mountains of Virginia and North Carolina. Along its nearly 217 miles in Virginia, you can watch sublime sunsets, scan for wildlife and lose all sense of the present while gazing at the vast wilderness. Hikes take you deeper into nature, from easy lakeside trails to challenging scrambles to soaring heights. Extend your visit by overnighting at a campsite or forest lodge.

Civil War Sites

Hallowed ground that transformed the nation

Battlegrounds (p72) are scattered across Maryland, West Virginia, Virginia and into Pennsylvania. Infamous sites connect you with some of America's darkest hours, when thousands perished during bloody pitched battles. Excellent on-site museums add historical context to the warfare, though nothing quite compares to walking the fields where these paradigm-shifting events unfolded. In summer you can witness (or join in) historical reenactments, including the Battle of Gettysburg.

National Mall & Memorial Parks

The monument-filled epicenter of Washington, DC

Almost 2 miles long and lined with iconic monuments and hallowed marble buildings, the National Mall (p82) is the epicenter of political and cultural life in Washington, DC. America's finest museums line the green, welcoming visitors year-round. There's no better place to learn about US history, whether you're tracing your hand along the Vietnam Veterans Memorial or ascending the steps of the Lincoln Memorial, where Dr Martin Luther King Jr gave his famous 'I Have a Dream' speech.

New River Gorge National Park

Rafting, hiking, camping and exploring ghost towns

Named a national park in 2020, this park (p88) is a wilderness beauty of forest-covered ridges, gushing waterfalls and wildlife-filled woodlands. Carving through this rugged landscape is the New River, one of the oldest waterways on the planet. There's much to do here, from white-water rafting the Gauley River to hiking to lofty clifftops overlooking the gorge. You can also explore human history, visiting ghostly boom towns as well as mining camps that have been reclaimed by the forest.

7

Cape Cod National Seashore

Pristine beaches and diverse coastal ecosystems

Breathe in the salty air while listening to the waves lapping the shore on glacier-formed Cape Cod (p50). Long before John F Kennedy added it to the national park system in 1961, the sandy peninsula drew artists, writers and philosophers, including Henry David Thoreau, who found inspiration here. Apart from ruminating on evocative sunrises and sunsets, the Cape is ideal for exploring protected wetlands, marshes, ponds and other features that are disappearing from many other parts of the US coastline.

RONALD WILSON PHOTOGRAPHY/GETTY IMAGES ©

CARLOS RESTREPO/
SHUTTERSTOCK ©

National Parks of New York Harbor

Nature and history on the edge of the metropolis

On the fringes of the most populated city in the US, you'll find surprising places to connect with nature (p56). Golden beaches, tidal flats and mixed woodlands all lie within easy reach of NYC. Plant and animal life proliferate here, from unusual blooms (like the eastern prickly pear cactus) to migratory birds that pass over by the millions during the spring and fall. NY Harbor is also where you can delve into the past at historic sites like the Statue of Liberty and Ellis Island.

Plan Your Trip
Need to Know

When to Go

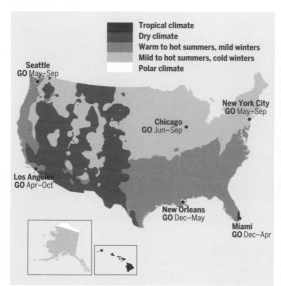

Tropical climate
Dry climate
Warm to hot summers, mild winters
Mild to hot summers, cold winters
Polar climate

Seattle
GO May–Sep

New York City
GO May–Sep

Chicago
GO Jun–Sep

Los Angeles
GO Apr–Oct

New Orleans
GO Dec–May

Miami
GO Dec–Apr

High Season (Jun–early Sep)

• Best time for outdoors, including hiking and cycling.

• Expect summertime crowds.

Shoulder (April, May & mid-Sep–Oct)

• Springtime blooms on the hills and mountains.

• Fall brings fiery colors (and crowds) to the woodlands.

• April/May are still cold in Acadia; many places remain closed.

Low Season (Nov–Mar)

• Carriage roads in Acadia transform into cross-country ski trails. Go snowshoeing on many trails.

• Many lodging options and restaurants near Acadia close for the season.

• All parks stay open; beware ice and wintery conditions on roads and trails.

Entry Fees

Acadia and Shenandoah: seven-day pass free or per vehicle/pedestrian from $30/15. New River Gorge: admission free.

America the Beautiful Annual Pass

$80 per vehicle valid for all national parks for 12 months from the date of purchase. Purchase online via National Park Service (www.nps.gov).

ATMs

ATMs are available in gateway towns.

Credit Cards

Major credit cards are widely accepted.

Cell Phones

Coverage inside parks is spotty at best.

Wi-fi

Once you enter the wilderness, there is no public wi-fi available. Outside the parks, most cafes and hotels offer free wi-fi.

Tipping

Tip restaurant servers 15–20%; porters $2 per bag; hotel housekeepers $2 to $5 per night.

Daily Costs

Budget: Less than $150
- Camping & RV sites: $30–50
- Park entrance fee: free–$30
- Self-catering food or cafe/diner meal: $8–20
- Park shuttles in Acadia: free

Midrange: $160–250
- Double room in midrange hotel: $120–200
- Popular restaurant dinner for two: $50–80
- Car hire per day: from $45

Top End: More than $250
- Double room in a top-end hotel: from $200
- Dinner in a top restaurant: $60–100
- Full-day rafting trip: from $100

Advance Planning

Six months before Reserve campsites or hotel rooms in satellite towns if visiting in summer. Book flights and reserve rental car if needed.

Two months before Reserve campsites if staying in Acadia (reservations available 60 days in advance). Book rafting trips and other guided excursions.

One month before If planning a long drive with your own car, take it in for a safety inspection and tune-up. If you're planning on hiking, start walking to get prepared.

Useful Websites

Lonely Planet (www.lonelyplanet.com/usa) Destination information, hotel bookings, traveler forum and more.

National Park Service (NPS; www.nps.gov) Hikes, campsites and expert advice.

Nothing But New England (www.nothingbutnewengland.com) Wide-ranging tips on activities and sights.

Accommodations

Campsites Reservations available at Shenandoah six months in advance and at Acadia up to two months in advance. New River Gorge's campsites (primitive only) are first-come, first-served. Flush toilets are available at most sites, hot showers are not. Full hookups for RVs are usually found outside parks.

Park Lodges & Cabins Shenandoah has some well-placed lodges and cabins that range from rustic to quite comfortable. Most are pet-friendly and some have wi-fi.

B&Bs Available in gateway towns outside parks; often excellent; usually include wi-fi.

Hotels & Resorts Found in gateway towns like Bar Harbor. The best have excellent amenities and views of the water.

Arriving at a National Park

Information Pick up a park newspaper at the entry kiosk and hang onto it; they're packed with useful information.

Camping If you want to camp at a first-come, first-served site, head straight to the campground. Try to arrive no later than mid-morning Friday.

Parking People not spending the night inside a park will find parking difficult. Arrive early. If visiting Acadia, park and take the free shuttle if possible.

Visitor Centers Best places to start exploring the parks. Purchase books and maps, ask rangers questions, check weather reports and trail and road conditions.

Getting Around

Car Most convenient way to travel between the parks. Traffic leading into and within the parks can be horrendous.

Park Shuttles Acadia has an excellent shuttle system with stops at major visitor sites and trailheads.

Bicycles Some gateway towns like Bar Harbor have rentals. Good for getting around developed areas and cycling carriage roads. Some shuttles transport bikes.

Plan Your Trip
Month by Month

January

Strap on your snowshoes or cross-country skis and enjoy the white winter magic in Acadia. With the right gear, you can also enjoy hiking amid the enchanting frozen landscapes of Shenandoah, New River Gorge and other forested areas.

March

The biting cold of winter is slowly fading, at least at lower elevations. The first spring blossoms appear in the southern reaches, while Acadia and much of New England lies snowbound.

🌸 National Cherry Blossom Festival

The star of Washington, DC's annual calendar celebrates spring's arrival with boat rides in the Tidal Basin, evening walks by lantern light, cultural fairs and a parade. The three-week event, from late March to mid-April, also commemorates Japan's gift of 3000 cherry trees in 1912.

🏃 Blossom Kite Festival

On the last Saturday of March, the skies near the Washington Monument come alive with color as kite lovers swoop on the National Mall. It's part of the National Cherry Blossom Festival.

April

Wildflowers are in full bloom at lower elevations, especially at Shenandoah, the New River Gorge and along the Appalachian Trail, and waterfalls begin pumping at full force with the beginning of the snowmelt. It's also a great time to grab your binoculars and watch the spring migration, when millions of birds make the northbound journey.

🏃 National Park Week

For one week in April, national parks host special programs and events. Early in the year, the US president announces when National Park Week will take place.

Above: National Cherry Blossom Festival

FILPHOTO/GETTY IMAGES ©

May

Visitors are slowly beginning to trickle into Acadia and Cape Cod, while hikers in southern Appalachia will enjoy some of the best conditions for outdoor adventures.

June

It's still possible to beat the crowds of summer in early June, though you'll need to hit the road (or trail) early in the day. By late June, the parks are jammed but the weather is stellar in many of them.

Summer Events at the Seashore

From June through August, catch free indoor and outdoor events at the National Seashore on Cape Cod. You can hear symphony concerts, jazz groups, funk bands, bluegrass and other styles, along with talks given by marine biologists and conservationists. Events take place at the Salt Pond Visitor Center in Eastham.

★ Best Events

National Park Week, April

National Cherry Blossom Festival, March

Summer Events at the Seashore, June to August

Reenactment of the Battle of Gettysburg, July

Foliage Season, October

✿ Smithsonian Folklife Festival

For 10 days around Independence Day, this extravaganza celebrates international and US cultures on the National Mall. The fest highlights a diverse mix of countries through folk music, dance, crafts, storytelling and international food.

Above: Smithsonian Folklife Festival

July

Steamy summer days are here, meaning it's a great time to cool off in the water. Cape Cod, Echo Lake or Sand Beach in Acadia, and hidden swimming holes around the region are the places to be.

Reenactment of the Battle of Gettysburg

In early July each year, hundreds of Civil War history buffs turn up to watch – or join in – the reenactment of the Battle of Gettysburg, which typically happens at Daniel Lady Farm (www.danielladyfarm.com).

Independence Day

Wherever you roam, you won't be far from a big fireworks show on July 4. Washington, DC, goes all out as huge crowds gather along Constitution Ave to watch marching bands parade and hear the Declaration of Independence read from the National Archives steps. Later the National Symphony Orchestra plays a concert on the Capitol's West Lawn, followed by mega fireworks over the National Mall.

Mashpee Wampanoag Powwow

On Cape Cod over the July 4th weekend, the Wampanoag sponsor the Mashpee Wampanoag Powwow, a big three-day event that includes Native American dancing, drumming, games, food and art, plus an awe-inspiring fireball ceremony after the sun sets on the Saturday evening. The event is held at the Cape's fairgrounds in East Falmouth.

August

Hello crowds! It's the height of summer, it's blazing hot, and every hotel and campsite is reserved. First-come, first-served campgrounds are your best bet. Be sure to include some stops at refreshing swimming holes to keep cool.

Provincetown Carnival

Held in the third week in August, Carnival in Provincetown, Cape Cod, is a week of fun-filled dance parties and streets filled with people in glorious, colorful costumes.

October

One of the most enchanting times to travel here, October brings fiery autumn blazes to the trails and scenic drives.

Foliage Season

Witness Mother Nature at her most ostentatious as the trees take on shades of red, gold and amber. The colors all around the region are dazzling, but especially as they blanket the mountainsides on Skyline Drive, along the Blue Ridge Parkway, across the New River Gorge and everywhere in Shenandoah.

Bridge Day Festival

On the third Saturday in October, hundreds of BASE jumpers parachute from the 876ft-high New River Gorge Bridge. See live music in Fayetteville the same weekend.

Wellfleet Oyster Days

If you're heading to Cape Cod National Seashore in October, don't miss this seafood-loving gathering in Wellfleet. This huge event the weekend after Columbus Day has plenty of eating, drinking and slurping.

November

Bar Harbor and other towns around Acadia close up for the season, with winter creeping in quickly. The parks are still open, however, making it a fine time to enjoy nature without the crowds.

December

Winter is well under way in the parks. Access roads are generally open, although the Park Loop Road in Acadia closes (apart from Ocean Drive and Jordan Pond Road, which remain open). Visitor centers typically remain closed.

National Audubon Society Christmas Bird Count

Every year around Christmastime, thousands of people take to the wilds to look for and record birds for the Audubon Society's annual survey. Many of the parks organize a count and rely on volunteers to help. Check the National Park Service website (www.nps.gov) for information.

Plan Your Trip
Get Inspired

WERKSMEDIA/GETTY IMAGES ©

Books

○ **Our National Parks**
(1901) The words of John Muir inspired a nation to embrace national parks.

○ **Canoeing in the Wilderness** (1857) Thoreau's account of traveling untamed landscapes in New England.

○ **Ranger Confidential** (2010) Former park ranger Andrea Lankford gives the inside scoop on park life.

○ **An American Sunrise** (2019) Personal and mournful poems of Native American culture by Joy Harjo.

○ **Our Southern Highlanders** (1913) Horace Kephart's fascinating and at times comical portraits of Appalachian peoples.

Films

○ **The National Parks: America's Best Idea** (2009) Ken Burns' fascinating 12-hour PBS miniseries delves into the groundbreaking history behind the creation of America's national parks.

○ **A Walk in the Woods** (2014) A rollicking, man-vs-nature tale of two aging friends tackling the Appalachian Trail.

○ **Gettysburg** (1993) The story of one of America's bloodiest battles and the turning point of the Civil War.

○ **American Experience: Ansel Adams** (2004) Inspire your snapshots with this PBS documentary.

Music

○ **Genuine Negro Jig** (2010) Brilliantly lyrical old-time bluegrass by African American string band Carolina Chocolate Drops.

○ **Poems, Prayers & Promises** (1971) John Denver's greatest album includes hits like 'Take Me Home, Country Roads', which became the anthem for West Virginia.

○ **What's Going on?** (1971) A masterpiece of soulful social commentary by Marvin Gaye.

○ **This Land is Your Land: The Asch Recordings, Vol. 1** (1997) Woody Guthrie sings everything from 'This Land is Your Land' to 'The Car Song.'

Above: Blue Ridge Mountains from the Appalachian Trail

Plan Your Trip
Health & Safety

Before You Go

If you require medications bring them in their original, labeled containers. A signed and dated letter from your physician describing your medical conditions and medications, including generic names, is a good idea. If carrying syringes or needles, be sure to have a physician's letter documenting their necessity.

Some national park walks are physically demanding and most require a reasonable level of fitness. Even if you're tackling the easy or easy-to-moderate walks, it pays to be relatively fit, rather than launch straight into them after months of fairly sedentary living. If you're aiming for the demanding walks, fitness is essential.

If you have any medical problems, or are concerned about your health in any way, it's a good idea to have a full checkup before you start walking.

In the Parks

Visiting city dwellers will need to keep their wits about them in order to minimize the chances of suffering an avoidable accident or tragedy. Dress appropriately, tell people where you are going, don't bite off more than you can chew and, above all, respect the wilderness and the inherent dangers that it conceals.

Crime is far more common in big cities than in sparsely populated national parks. Nevertheless, use common sense: lock valuables in the trunk of your vehicle, and never leave anything worth stealing in your tent.

Environmental Hazards

o Poisonous Plants Poison ivy is widely present in the park. Learn to recognize its three-leaf pattern. Vines may not be easy to identify, and should be avoided.

o Ticks Wear long sleeves and pants to protect from ticks. Always check your body for ticks after walking through high grass or thickly forested areas. If ticks are found unattached, they can simply be brushed off. If a tick is found attached, press down around the tick's head with tweezers, grab the head and gently pull upward – do not twist it. (If no tweezers are available, use your fingers.) Don't douse an attached tick with oil, alcohol or petroleum jelly. Tick-borne diseases, such as Lyme disease, are an increasing worry. If you become ill after receiving the bite, seek medical treatment immediately. Tick bites can occur any time of year, though infections are more common in the warm-weather months from May to September.

o **Venomous Snakes** There are several venomous snakes in the region, including copperheads and timber rattlesnakes. These snakes are not aggressive and prefer to avoid humans. Most bites occur from people stepping on an unnoticed snake. Those bitten will experience local pain and swelling. Death is rare even without treatment.

Hypothermia

This life-threatening condition occurs when prolonged exposure to cold thwarts the body's ability to maintain its core temperature. Hypothermia is a real danger, regardless of the season. Cold, wet and wind can form a deadly combination, even with temperatures in the 50°Fs (10°C to 15°C). At higher elevations, hypothermia can occur even in the summer.

Symptoms include uncontrolled shivering, poor muscle control and irrational behavior. Treat symptoms by putting dry clothing on the victim, giving them warm fluids and warming them through direct body contact with another person. Prevention is the best strategy: remember to dress in layers and wear a waterproof, windproof outer jacket.

Walk Safety: Basic Rules

o Allow plenty of time to accomplish a walk before dark, particularly when daylight hours are shorter.

o Study the route carefully before setting out, noting possible escape routes and the point of no return (where it's quicker to continue than turn back). Monitor your progress during the day against the time estimated for the walk, and keep an eye on the weather.

★ Water Purification

To ensure you are getting safe, clean drinking water in the backcountry you have three basic options:

Boiling Water is considered safe to drink if it has been boiled at 100°C for at least a minute. This is best done when you set up your camp and stove in the evening.

Chemical Purification There are two types of chemical additives that will purify water: chlorine or iodine. You can choose from various products on the market. Read instructions carefully first, be aware of expiration dates and check you are not allergic to either chemical.

Filtration Mobile devices can pump water through microscopic filters and take out potentially harmful organisms. If carrying a filter, take care it doesn't get damaged in transit, read the instructions carefully and always filter the cleanest water you can find.

o It's wise not to walk alone. Always leave details of your intended route, number of people in your group and expected return time with someone responsible before you set off, and let them know when you return.

o Before setting off, make sure you have a relevant map, compass and whistle, and that you know the weather forecast for the area for the next 24 hours.

Rescue & Evacuation

If a person in your group is injured, leave someone with them while others seek help. If there are only two of you, leave the injured person with as much warm clothing, food and water as it's sensible to spare, plus a whistle and flashlight. Mark their position with something conspicuous.

Above left: Appalachian Mountains

Plan Your Trip
Clothing & Equipment

Deciding what gear you need for a trip and what will only weigh you down is an art. Don't forget essentials, but be ruthless when packing, since every ounce counts when you're lugging your gear up a steep hillside. Smartphone apps, new filtration systems and battery chargers are changing the game.

Layering

The secret to comfortable walking is to wear several layers of light clothing, which you can easily take off or put on as you warm up or cool down. Most walkers use three main layers: a base layer next to the skin, an insulating layer, and an outer-shell layer for protection from wind, rain and snow.

For the upper body, the base layer is typically a shirt of synthetic material that wicks moisture away from the body and reduces chilling. The insulating layer retains heat next to your body, and is usually a (windproof) fleece jacket or sweater. The outer shell consists of a waterproof jacket that also protects against cold wind.

For the lower body, the layers generally consist of either shorts or loose-fitting trousers, thermal underwear ('long johns') and waterproof overtrousers.

When purchasing outdoor clothing, one of the most practical fabrics is merino wool. Though pricier than other materials, natural wool absorbs sweat, retains heat even when wet, and is soft and comfortable to wear. Even better, it doesn't store odors like other sports garments, so you can wear it for several days in a row without inflicting antisocial smells on your tent mates.

Waterproof Shells

Jackets should be made of a breathable, waterproof fabric, with a hood that is roomy enough to cover headwear, but that still allows peripheral vision. Other handy features include underarm zippers for easy ventilation and a large map pocket with a heavy-gauge zipper protected by a storm flap. Waterproof pants are best with slits for pocket access and long leg zips so that you can pull them on and off over your boots.

Footwear

Running shoes are OK for walks that are graded easy or moderate. However, you'll probably appreciate, if not need, the support and protection provided by hiking boots for more demanding walks. Nonslip soles (such as Vibram) provide the best grip.

Buy boots in warm conditions or go for a walk before trying them on, so that your feet can expand slightly, as they would on a hike. It's also a good idea to carry a pair of sandals to wear at night for getting in and out of tents easily or at rest stops. Sandals are also useful when fording waterways.

Gaiters help to keep your feet dry in wet weather and on boggy ground; they can also deflect small stones or sand and maintain leg warmth. The best are made of strong fabric, with a robust zip protected by a flap, and secure easily around the foot.

Walking socks should be free of ridged seams in the toes and heels.

Backpacks & Daypacks

For day walks, a daypack (30L to 40L) will usually suffice, but for multiday walks you will need a backpack of between 45L and 90L capacity. Even if the manufacturer claims your pack is waterproof, use heavy-duty liners.

Tent

A three-season tent will fulfill most walkers' requirements. The floor and the outer shell, or fly, should have taped or sealed seams and covered zips to stop leaks. The weight can be as low as 2.2lb (1kg) for a stripped-down, low-profile tent, and up to 6.6lb (3kg) for a luxury, four-season model. Dome- and tunnel-shaped tents handle windy conditions better than flat-sided tents.

Emergency Supplies

Pack a first-aid kit and know what's in it. At a minimum, you'll want antiseptic wipes, bandages, gauze pads, medical tape and antibacterial ointment to treat cuts, scrapes and blisters. It should also include pain-relief medication (eg ibuprofen), insect sting relief, antihistamine, tweezers and a pocket knife (or other multi-tool). Don't forget to pack epinephrine if you're allergic to insect stings, and bring other meds you might need (an inhaler if you have asthma, pre-filled insulin pens if you have diabetes etc).

Some hikers travel with bear pepper spray. If you choose to bring it, make sure you know how to use it, and keep it handy (in arm's reach, not stuffed in the bottom of your backpack).

Hiking Gear

A good walking stick or two lightweight ski poles will come in handy while hiking challenging uphill and downhill trails.

Even if you intend to complete your hike before nightfall, take a flashlight just in case something happens and you can't make it back before sunset.

Map & Compass

Always carry a good map of the area in which you are walking, and know how to read it. Buy a compass and learn how to use it. Make sure your compass is balanced for your destination zone. There are also 'universal' compasses on the market that can be used anywhere in the world.

Other useful items include an emergency Mylar blanket, a whistle and signal mirror for attracting attention, and a fire starter (for an emergency survival fire).

Above left: Bar Harbor

Plan Your Trip

New England & Mid-Atlantic National Parks Overview

NAME	STATE	ENTRANCE FEE
Acadia National Park (p38)	Maine	7-day pass per vehicle $30
New River Gorge National Park (p88)	West Virginia	Free
Shenandoah National Park (p62)	Virginia	7-day pass per vehicle $30

Other NPS-Designated Sites & Areas

NAME	STATE	DESIGNATION
Antietam National Battlefield (p72)	Maryland	National Battlefield
Appomattox Court House (p77)	Virginia	National Historical Park
Boston Harbor Islands National Recreation Area (p79)	Massachusetts	National Recreation Area
Cape Cod National Seashore (p82)	Massachusetts	National Seashore
Contrabands & Freedmen Cemetery (p79)	Virginia	National Register of Historic Places
Fredericksburg & Spotsylvania National Military Park (p74)	Virginia	National Battlefield Park
Gettysburg National Military Park (p80)	Pennsylvania	National Military Park
Harriet Tubman Underground Railroad National Historic Park (p78)	Maryland	National Historical Park

DESCRIPTION	GREAT FOR...
The only national park in New England encompasses an unspoiled wilderness of undulating coastal mountains, towering sea cliffs, surf-pounded beaches and quiet ponds.	
The National Park Service protects a stretch of the New River that falls 750ft over 50 miles. The region is an adventure mecca, with world-class white-water rafting and hiking trails with beautiful views.	
In spring and summer the wildflowers explode; in fall the leaves burn bright; and in winter a beautiful hibernation period sets in.	

DESCRIPTION

The Battle of Antietam, fought in Sharpsburg, MD, on September 17, 1862, has the dubious distinction of marking the bloodiest day in American history.

Where the Confederacy finally surrendered.

Georges Island, in the Boston Harbor Islands National Recreation Area, is the site of Fort Warren, a 19th-century fort and Civil War prison.

Cape Cod National Seashore is a treasure trove of protected unspoiled beaches, dunes, salt marshes, nature trails and forests.

During the Civil War, the Union-controlled Southern city of Alexandria, VA, became a safe haven for formerly enslaved African Americans. Some 1800 contrabands (as freed slaves were called) and freedmen were buried at this cemetery.

More than 13,000 Americans were killed during the Civil War in four battles fought in a 17-mile radius covered by this park: Fredericksburg, Chancellorsville, the Wilderness and Spotsylvania Courthouse.

The Battle of Gettysburg, fought in Gettysburg, PA, in July of 1863, marked the turning point of the Civil War and the high-water mark of the Confederacy's attempted rebellion.

This visitor center and historic site honors Harriet Tubman, 'the Moses of her people' who led black slaves to freedom on the Underground Railroad, the pipeline that sent escaped slaves north.

NAME	STATE	DESIGNATION
Manassas National Battlefield Park (p74)	Virginia	National Battlefield Park
Monocacy National Battlefield (p78)	Maryland	National Battlefield
National Mall & Memorial Parks (p82)	Washington, DC	National Memorials, Monuments and Historic Sites
National Parks of New York Harbor (p56)	New York	National Memorials, Monuments, Historic Sites and Recreation Areas
Petersburg National Battlefield (p76)	Virginia	National Battlefield

Classic Road Trips

NAME	STATE	DISTANCE/DURATION
Across the Appalachian Trail (p92)	Maine–Georgia	495 miles / 5 days
Blue Ridge Parkway (p98)	Virginia and North Carolina	185 miles / 3 days
Civil War Tour (p72)	Maryland–Virginia	150 miles / 3–4 days
Skyline Drive (p66)	Virginia	150 miles / 3 days

DESCRIPTION

The site of the first major pitched battle of the Civil War.

The crucial but little known Battle of Monocacy occurred during the last Confederate invasion of the North.

National Mall and Memorial Parks protects 14 sites on the mall, as well as other memorials in downtown Washington, DC.

There are 11 sites managed by the National Park Service surrounding the port of New York City, preserving more than 400 years of American history.

Marks the spot where Northern and Southern soldiers spent almost a quarter of the Civil War in a protracted, entrenched standoff.

DESCRIPTION	ESSENTIAL PHOTO
The Appalachian Trail runs 2175 miles from Maine to Georgia, across the original American frontier and some of the oldest mountains on the continent. It is today managed as a National Scenic Trail.	The New River Gorge Bridge from the visitor center trail.
The Blue Ridge National Scenic Byway is the most visited area of national parkland in the USA. This trip threads into and off the parkway.	A panorama of the Blue Ridge Mountains from Sharp Top, Peaks of Otter.
On this trip you'll cross battlefields where more than 100,000 Americans perished and are buried, foe beside foe; many of the battlefields are now preserved by the National Park Service, amid rolling farmlands, sunny hills and deep forests.	The fences and fields of Antietam at sunset.
The centerpiece of the ribbon-thin Shenandoah National Park is the jaw-dropping beauty of Skyline Drive, which runs for just over 100 miles atop the Blue Ridge Mountains.	The fabulous 360-degree horizon at the top of Bearfence Mountain.

Plan Your Trip
Best Hiking

Above: Old Rag Mountain; Top left: Endless Wall Trail; Top right: Cadillac Mountain

Nothing encapsulates the spirit of the national parks like hiking. You'll find countless trails in New England and the Mid-Atlantic that offer access to craggy mountain overlooks, picturesque waterfalls and wildlife-filled forests.

Appalachian Trail

One of the world's most famous routes crosses 14 states and takes you along dramatic ridge lines and through primeval forests. Access it in Shenandoah or the Blue Ridge Parkway.

Cadillac Mountain

There are various ways to reach the highest peak in Acadia National Park, with exhilarating views along the way. Up top, don't miss the family-friendly Summit Loop, a magical place to be at sunrise or sunset.

Endless Wall Trail

Enjoy every shade of green imaginable (except in fall when the trees are ablaze) as you enjoy the views over a magnificent stretch of the New River.

Old Rag Mountain

Feel like you're on top of the world after the challenging ascent to this craggy summit in Shenandoah, where you'll have 360-degree views over undulating Appalachian peaks.

Plan Your Trip
Best Wildlife Watching

Above: Black bears, Shenandoah National Park; Top right: Falcon, Gateway National Recreation Area;
Bottom right: Harbor Seal, Chatham Fish Pier

From tiny pygmy shrews to school-bus-sized whales, the northeast harbors an astonishing variety of wildlife. Wherever you roam, try to time your visits for dawn or dusk to maximize your chances of animal encounters.

Chatham Harbor

Part of the Cape Cod National Seashore, this scenic harbor is a great place to see harbor seals. Head to Chatham Fish Pier to watch them surrounding fishing boats as they dock.

Big Meadows

Bears are a possibility anywhere along Skyline Drive, though the section south of Big Meadows often has the most frequent sightings. It's also a prime place to see white-tailed deer.

Jordan Pond

Take it slow as you walk around this glacier-formed pond in Acadia and you may spot beavers swimming along the shore as well as their handiwork of beaver lodges and felled trees.

Gateway National Recreation Area

The wetlands near NYC are among the best places in the northeast to look for migratory birds, with over 300 species passing through each year.

Hawksbill Summit

Home to some of the best scenery in Shenandoah, the Hawksbill area is also a big draw for spotting unique wildlife, including foxes and flocks of wild turkeys.

Plan Your Trip
Best Family Experiences

Above: Rose River; Top left: Luray Caverns; Top right: Sand Beach

Pulling kids (and adults) off their screens and into a national park can be a transformative experience. It's also a great chance for the whole family to enjoy some time outdoors, whether checking out waterfalls or looking for stars in pollution-free night skies.

Luray Caverns

Attracting visitors since its discovery in the 19th century, this 400-million-year-old subterranean wonderland is the largest cave on the East Coast.

Sand Beach

Bask by the shore by day, then return at night to hear rangers tell stories and point out constellations during the Stars Over Sand Beach program in Acadia.

Lewis Mountain Campground

Roast marshmallows on the campfire while watching fireflies and listening to the nighttime creatures of the forest at this peaceful campground in Shenandoah.

Province Lands Bike Trail

Rent bikes and go for a spin on this vehicle-free greenway through forest and past dunes on Cape Cod. Outfitters in Provincetown rent a variety of bicycles including kids bikes, trailers and tag-a-longs

Rose River Loop

Make the 4-mile round-trip hike to see a picturesque waterfall, with inviting swimming holes along the way.

Plan Your Trip
Best Adventures

Above: Witch Hole Pond; Top right: Gauley River; Bottom right: Precipice Trail

Plunging gorges, rushing white-water rapids and clifftop heights set the stage for adrenaline fueled activities. You can also plan a winter trip for adventures in the snow.

Rafting the Gauley River

Feel the rush as you and your wave-battered raft mates bounce and glide along a thundering stretch of the Gauley River. Come during the fall release for the ride of your life.

Gorge Adventures

Hop on a mountain bike (best hired from nearby Fayetteville) and hit these rugged loops in the New River Gorge Area. You can choose from four different routes, which take you through forests on roller-coaster-style single track.

Precipice Trail

No ropes are necessary, just steely resolve to hike this cliffside trail in Acadia. You'll ascend Champlain Mountain along slender ledges and up granite walls (with the help of strategically placed iron rungs) for a sweeping view over mountain and sea at the top.

Carriage Roads

When the chilly winds arrive, Acadia's 45 miles of carriage roads become an enchanting wintery backdrop to cross-country skiing. Hit Witch Hole Pond Loop for an easy outing or Amphitheater Loop for more of a challenge.

NEW ENGLAND & THE MID-ATLANTIC

SKYLER EWING/SHUTTERSTOCK ©

Acadia National Park

The only national park in New England encompasses an unspoiled wilderness of undulating coastal mountains, towering sea cliffs, surf-pounded beaches and quiet ponds. Swimmers can brave the chilly waters, hikers will delight in 125 miles of trails, and summer brings ranger programs and stargazing sessions.

Great For...

State
Maine

Entrance Fee
7-day pass per car/motorcycle/person on foot or bicycle $30/25/15

Area
73 sq miles

❶ Park Loop Road

Unfurling for 27 gorgeous miles, Park Loop Rd is the main sightseeing jaunt through the park. On the portion called Ocean Dr, stop at lovely **Sand Beach**, and at **Thunder Hole** for a look at the surf crashing into a cleft in the granite. The effect is most dramatic with a strong incoming tide.

Otter Cliff, not far south of Thunder Hole, is basically a wall of pink granite rising right out from the sea. This area is popular with rock climbers.

The road is largely one way; in summer you can cover the route on the Island Explorer bus system (shuttle route 4; www.exploreacadia.com). Note that the loop road is closed in winter, and its opening may be delayed by heavy snow.

Previous page: Acadia National Park
LUKAS PROSZOWSKI/SHUTTERSTOCK ©

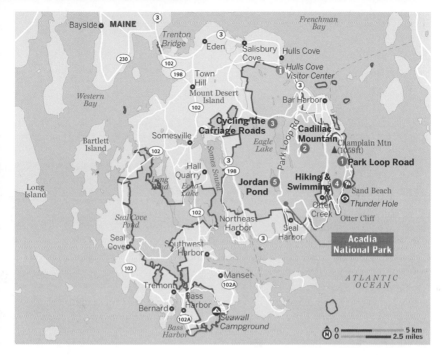

❷ Cadillac Mountain

Don't leave the park without driving – or hiking – to the 1530ft summit of Cadillac Mountain. For panoramic views of Frenchman Bay, walk the paved 0.5-mile **Cadillac Mountain Summit Loop**. The summit is a popular place in the early morning because it's long been touted as the first spot in the US to see the sunrise. The truth? It is, but only between October 7 and March 6. The crown is passed to northern coastal towns the rest of the year because of the tilt of the earth. But, hey, the sunset is always a good bet.

❸ Cycling the Carriage Roads

John D Rockefeller Jr, a lover of old-fashioned horse carriages, gifted Acadia with some 45 miles of crisscrossing carriage roads. Made from crushed stone, the roads are free from cars and are popular with cyclists, hikers and equestrians. Several of them fan out from Jordan

Pond House, but if the lot is too crowded continue north to the parking area at **Eagle Lake** on US 233 to link to the carriage road network.

The Bicycle Express Shuttle runs to Eagle Lake from the Bar Harbor Village Green from late June through September. Pick up a *Carriage Road User's Map* at the visitor center.

❹ Hiking & Swimming

Acadia has more than 125 miles of trails. Some are easy enough to stroll with a small child, while others require sturdy boots, full water bottles and plenty of lung power. The Cadillac Mountain Summit Loop is an easy choice, and a good moderate pick is the forested 2.2-mile trail to the summit of **Champlain Mountain**. A little further south, the **Beehive Trail** (p48), at less than a mile, involves clinging to iron rings bolted to the cliff face and is for the fit.

Near the Beehive trailhead, swimmers can brave the icy (55°F, even in midsummer!) waters of **Sand Beach** or take a dip in the marginally warmer **Echo Lake**, west of Somes Sound. Both areas have lifeguard patrols in summer.

⑤ Jordan Pond

On clear days, the glassy waters of this 176-acre pond reflect the image of Penobscot Mountain like a mirror. A stroll around the pond and its surrounding forests and flower meadows is one of Acadia's most popular and family-friendly activities. (Sorry, no swimming allowed.) Follow the 3-mile self-guided nature trail around the pond before stopping for a cuppa at the Jordan Pond House (p42).

Essential Information

Sleeping

Most of the hotels, B&Bs and private campgrounds are in Bar Harbor. There are two great rustic campgrounds in the Mt Desert Island section of the park, with around 500 tent sites between them. Both are densely wooded but only a few minutes' walk to the ocean.

Note that reservations for the park campgrounds are handled by Recreation. gov, not the park itself.

Seawall Campground (☎877-444-6777; www. recreation.gov; 668 Seawall Rd; tent sites $22-30, RV sites $30; ☺late May-Sep) Four miles south of Southwest Harbor, Seawall has 200 sites (no electric hookups). There are flush toilets, running water, a dump station, picnic tables and fire rings. Paid showers and a campers store are 1 mile away. Reservations are essential.

Eating

Picnickers will find plenty of areas to enjoy alfresco dining – bring supplies from Bar Harbor.

Jordan Pond House (☎207-276-3316; https:// jordanpondhouse.com; Park Loop Rd; tea & popovers $11, mains $11-33; ☺11am-9pm mid-May–mid-Oct) Afternoon tea at this lodge-like teahouse has been an Acadia tradition since the late 1800s. Steaming pots of Earl Grey come with hot popovers (hollow rolls made with egg batter) and strawberry jam. The large lunch menu ranges from lobster quiche to meatloaf sandwich.

Visitor Center

The informative **Hulls Cove Visitor Center** (☎207-288-8832; www.nps.gov/acad; ME 3; ☺8:30am-4:30pm mid-Apr–Jun, Sep & Oct, 8am-6pm Jul & Aug) anchors the park's main Hulls Cove entrance, 3 miles northwest of Bar Harbor via ME 3. Buy your park pass and pick up maps and info. The 27-mile-long Park Loop Rd, which circumnavigates the eastern section of Mt Desert Island, starts near here.

When the visitor center is closed (November to mid-April), head to park headquarters, 3 miles west of Bar Harbor on ME 233, for information.

Getting Around

Hiring a bike in nearby Bar Harbor is a breeze, and a good way to avoid traffic snarls and parking problems.

The free shuttle system, the Island Explorer (www.exploreacadia.com), features nine routes that link hotels, inns and campgrounds to destinations within Acadia National Park. Route maps are available at local establishments and online. Most of the routes converge on the Village Green in Bar Harbor. The shuttle runs from late June to mid-October.

Top left: Sunrise from Cadillac Mountain; Top right: Hikers on Champlain Mountain; Bottom: Jordan Pond

CLASSIC ROAD TRIPS

Acadia National Park

John D Rockefeller Jr and other wealthy landowners gave Acadia its bridges, overlooks and stone steps. Travelers can put Rockefeller's planning to good use by touring the wonderful Park Loop Rd by car.

Duration 3 days

Distance 112 miles

Best Time to Go
May through October for good weather and open facilities.

Essential Photo
Capture that sea-and-sunrise panorama from atop Cadillac Mountain.

Best for Outdoors
Hike a 'ladder trail' up a challenging cliff.

❶ Hulls Cove Visitor Center
Whoa, whoa, whoa. Before zooming into Bar Harbor on ME 3, stop at the park visitor center (p42) to get the lay of the land and pay the admission fee. Inside, head directly to the large diorama, which provides a helpful overview of Mt Desert Island (MDI). As you'll see, Acadia National Park shares the island with several nonpark communities, which are tucked here and there beside Acadia's borders.

From the visitor center, the best initiation to the park is to drive the 27-mile **Park Loop Road**, which links the park's highlights in the eastern section of MDI. It's one way (traveling clockwise) for most of its length.

The Drive » From the visitor center, turn right onto the Park Loop Rd, not ME 3 (which leads into Bar Harbor). Take in a nice view of Frenchman Bay on your left before passing the spur to ME 233. A short distance ahead, turn left to begin the one-way loop on Park Loop Rd.

❷ Sieur de Monts Spring
Nature lovers and history buffs will enjoy a stop at the Sieur de Monts Spring area at the intersection of ME 3 and the Park Loop Rd. Here you'll find a nature center and the summer-only branch of the **Abbe Museum** (☎207-288-3519; www.abbemuseum.org; ME 3 & Park Loop Rd; adult/child $3/1; ⊙10am-5pm late May-Oct), which sits in a lush, nature-like setting and hosts a fascinating collection of natural artifacts related to Maine's Native American heritage. Twelve of Acadia's biospheres are displayed in miniature at the **Wild Gardens of Acadia** FREE, from bog to coniferous woods to meadow. Botany enthusiasts will appreciate the plant labels. There are also some amazing stone-step trails here, appearing out of the talus as if by magic.

The Drive » If you wish to avoid driving the full park loop, you can follow ME 3 from here into Bar Harbor. Push on for the full experience – you won't regret it.

❸ Precipice Trail
What's the most exciting way to get a bird's-eye view of the park? By climbing up to where the birds are. Two 'ladder trails' cling to the sides of exposed cliffs on the northeastern section of Park Loop Rd, dubbed Ocean Dr. If you're fit and the season's right, tackle the first of the ladder trails, the steep, challenging 1.6-mile Precipice Trail, which climbs the east face of Champlain Mountain on iron rungs and ladders. (Note that the trail is typically closed late spring to mid-August because it's a nesting area for peregrine falcons. If it is closed, you might find volunteers and staff monitoring the birds through scopes

from the trailhead parking lot.) Skip the trail on rainy days.

The Drive » Continue south on Park Loop Rd. The Beehive Trail starts 100ft north of the Sand Beach parking area.

❹ Beehive Trail & Sand Beach

Another good ladder trail is the Beehive Trail (p48). The 0.8-mile climb includes ladders, rungs, narrow wooden bridges and scrambling – with steep drop-offs. As with the Precipice Trail, it's recommended that you descend via a nearby walking route, rather than climbing down.

Don't let the crowds keep you away from Sand Beach. It's home to one of the few sandy shorelines in the park, and it's a don't-miss spot. But you don't have to visit in the middle of the day to appreciate its charms. Beat the crowds early in the morning, or visit at night, especially for the **Stars over Sand Beach** program. During these free one-hour talks, lie on the beach, look up at the sky and listen to rangers share

stories and science about the stars. Even if you miss the talk, the eastern coastline along Ocean Dr is worth checking out at night, when you can watch the Milky Way slip right into the ocean.

The Drive » Swoop south past the crashing waves of Thunder Hole. If you want to exit the loop road, turn right onto Otter Cliff Rd, which hooks up to ME 3 north into Bar Harbor. Otherwise, pass Otter Point then follow the road inland past Wildwood Stables.

❺ Jordan Pond House

Share hiking stories with other nature-lovers at the lodge-like Jordan Pond House (p42) over a traditional afternoon tea. If you catch clear weather, Mt Penobscot's mirror image is visible in the waters of Jordan Pond.

The Drive » Look up for the rock precariously perched atop South Bubble from the pull-off almost 2 miles north. Continue north to access Cadillac Mountain Rd.

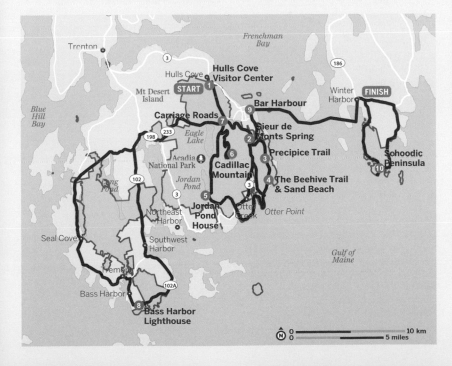

⑥ Cadillac Mountain

The summit of Cadillac Mountain is the first spot in the US to see the sunrise (well, between October 7 and March 6). Drink in the views of Frenchman Bay, whether or not you arise to greet the dawn.

The Drive » You could complete the loop road and exit the park, heading for your accommodations or next destination. But consider finding a parking lot and tackling walking trails, heading to Bar Harbor to hire bikes, or continuing on with your drive.

⑦ Carriage Roads

One of John D Rockefeller Jr's gifts to the park was 45 miles of carriage roads. Car-free and popular among cyclists, several such roads branch out from Jordan Pond House, or you can meet them a bit further north, here by Eagle Lake.

The Drive » Still in the mood for cruising? Before you head for the bright lights of Bar Harbor, take a detour: drive ME 233 toward the western part of MDI, connecting to ME 198 west, then drop south on ME 102 toward Southwest Harbor. Pass Echo Lake Beach and Southwest Harbor, then bear left onto ME 102A for a dramatic rise up and back into the park near the seawall.

⑧ Bass Harbor Head Lighthouse

There is only one lighthouse on Mt Desert Island, and it sits in the somnolent village of Bass Harbor in the far southwest corner of the park. Built in 1858, the 36ft lighthouse still has a Fresnel lens from 1902. It's in a beautiful location that's a photographer favorite. The lighthouse is a coastguard residence, so you can't go inside, but you can take photos. You can also stroll to the coast on two easy trails near the property: the **Ship Harbor Trail**, a 1.2-mile loop, and the **Wonderland Trail**, a 1.4-mile round trip. These trails are spectacular ways to get through the forest and to the coast, which looks different to the coast on Ocean Dr.

The Drive » For a lollipop loop, return on ME 102A to ME 102 through the village of Bass Harbor. Follow ME 102 then ME 233 all the way to Bar Harbor.

⑨ Bar Harbor

Tucked on the rugged coast in the shadows of Acadia's mountains, Bar Harbor is a busy gateway town with a J Crew joie de vivre. Restaurants, taverns and boutiques are scattered along Main St, Mt Desert St and Cottage St. Shops sell everything from books to camping gear to handicrafts and art. Visit this large branch of the **Abbe Museum** (26 Mt Desert St; adult/child $8/4; ⊙10am-5pm May-Oct, 10am-4pm Thu-Sat Nov-Apr). The collection holds more than 50,000 objects, such as pottery, tools, combs and fishing instruments spanning the last 2000 years, including contemporary pieces.

Done browsing? Spend the rest of the afternoon, or early evening, exploring the area by water. Sign up in Bar Harbor for a half-day or sunset sea-kayaking trip. **Coastal Kayaking Tours** (☎207-288-9605; www.acadiafun.com; 48 Cottage St; 2½hr/half-day tours $46/56; ⊙May-Oct) offers guided trips along the jagged coast.

The Drive » There's another part of the park you haven't yet explored. Reaching it involves a 44-mile drive (north on Rte 3 to US 1, following it about 17 miles to ME 186 S). ME 186 passes through Winter Harbor and then links to Schoodic Point Loop Rd. It's about an hour's drive one way. Alternatively, hop on a Downeast Windjammer ferry from the pier beside the Bar Harbor Inn.

⑩ Schoodic Peninsula

The Schoodic Peninsula is the only section of Acadia National Park that's part of the mainland. It's also home to the Schoodic Loop Rd, a rugged, woodsy drive with splendid views of Mt Desert Island and Cadillac Mountain. You're more likely to see a moose here than on MDI – what moose wants to cross a bridge?

Much of the drive is one way. There's an excellent **campground** (☎877-444-6777; www.recreation.gov; campsites $22-30; ⊙late

May–mid-Oct) near the entrance, then a picnic area at **Frazer Point**. Further along the loop, turn right for a short ride to **Schoodic Point**, a 440ft-high promontory with ocean views.

The full loop from Winter Harbor is 11.5 miles and covers park, town and state roads. If you're planning to come by ferry, you could rent a bike beforehand at **Bar Harbor Bicycle Shop** (✆207-288-3886; www.barharborbike.com; 141 Cottage St; rental per day $25-50; ⊗8am-6pm) – the loop road's smooth surface and easy hills make it ideal for cycling.

In July and August, the Island Explorer Schoodic shuttle bus runs from Winter Harbor to the peninsula ferry terminal and around the Park Loop Rd. It does not link to Bar Harbor.

Top: Wild Gardens of Acadia; Bottom: Bass Harbor Head Lighthouse

Hike Beehive Loop

FIREFLY, NEWENGLAND/SHUTTERSTOCK ©

Acadia has a handful of hikes that feel a bit like a European via ferrata, where you'll be ascending stretches of the trail with the help of iron, ladder-like rungs. Those with a fear of heights may want to skip this one.

Though it's not particularly long, the Beehive offers plenty of challenges. It's also quite popular, so set out early to avoid trail crowding. Start at the Bowl Trailhead, which is just north of Sand Beach (and about 4 miles south of Bar Harbor). After a third of a mile, the Bowl continues off to the left, and the Beehive Trail begins. You'll know you're on the right trail by the yellow warning sign describing the dangers of

Duration two hours

Distance 1.6 miles

Difficulty Hard

Start Bowl Trailhead

End Bowl Trailhead

this hike. Shortly after starting, you'll see the granite cliff rising up ahead. The trail goes right up the face of the mountain, and you'll soon find yourself climbing up steep sections along narrow exposed cliffs. At times, you'll have to scramble up iron-rung ladders along the mountain. Don't rush,

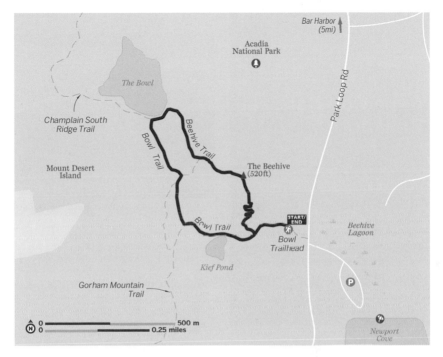

Bar Harbor
(5mi)

Acadia
National Park

The Bowl

Champlain South
Ridge Trail

Park Loop Rd

Bowl Trail

Beehive Trail

Mount Desert
Island

The Beehive
(520ft)

Bowl Trail

START/
END

Beehive
Lagoon

Bowl
Trailhead

Kief Pond

Gorham Mountain
Trail

P

500 m
0.25 miles

N

Newport
Cove

just take it slow – you'll likely have to stop often to wait for those climbing up ahead of you. After a few tough sections, you'll finally reach the summit. The views at the top are outstanding, with a sweeping panorama overlooking Frenchman Bay, Great Head and Sand Beach. This is a great place to enjoy a picnic lunch. From the top, it's a much easier descent. You'll continue along the Beehive Trail down the mountain, until you reach the Bowl, a spring-fed pond nestled amid the southern slopes of Champlain Mountain. From here you'll turn left and continue along the Bowl Trail, which will take you back to the Bowl Trailhead.

If you're game for more hiking, the Beehive connects with several other trails in the park, including Gorham Mountain Trail (heading south) and the Champlain South Ridge Trail (heading north).

Avoid making this hike after or during a rainstorm. The paths (and ladders) get slippery and can be quite hazardous. Ice can be a possibility from October to early May.

After the hike, head down to cool off in the chilly waters off Sand Beach.

If you enjoyed the thrill of the Beehive, take it to the next level and try the Precipice Trail, which is even longer, with equally challenging via ferrata–style stretches.

Cape Cod National Seashore

Cape Cod National Seashore extends some 40 miles around the curve of the Outer Cape and encompasses the Atlantic shoreline from Orleans all the way to Provincetown. Under the auspices of the National Park Service, it's a treasure trove of unspoiled beaches, dunes, salt marshes, nature trails and forests. Thanks to the backing of President John F Kennedy, this vast area was set aside for preservation in the 1960s, just before a building boom hit the rest of his native Cape Cod.

Marconi Beach

Marconi is a narrow Atlantic beach backed by sea cliffs and undulating dunes. It's named for famous Italian inventor Guglielmo Marconi, who sent the first transatlantic wireless message from a station nearby in 1903. The Atlantic White Cedar Swamp Trail is a 1.5-mile nature trail that's worth exploring.

JAMES KIRKIKIS /SHUTTERSTOCK ©

Highland Light

Sitting on the Cape's highest elevation (a mere 120ft!), Cape Cod Highland Light (www.capecodlight.org) dates to 1797 and casts the brightest beam on the New England coast. Admission includes a 10-minute video, an exhibit in the keeper's house and a climb up the lighthouse's 69 steps to a sweeping vista.

PATRICK MESSIER/SHUTTERSTOCK ©

Coast Guard Beach

All roads lead to Coast Guard Beach. The main road from the Salt Pond Visitor Center deposits you here, as do cycling and hiking trails. And it's for good reason: this grand beach, backed by a classic coast-guard station, is a stunner that attracts everyone from beachcombers to hard-core surfers. Bird-watchers also flock to Coast Guard Beach for the eagle-eye view of Nauset Marsh.

Nauset Light Beach

Cliff-backed Nauset Light Beach, north of Coast Guard Beach, is the stuff of dreams. It's broad and sandy and its features and facilities are similar to Coast Guard Beach, but there's a large parking lot right at the beach. A photogenic lighthouse guards the shoreline.

Herring Cove Beach

Swimmers favor the relatively calm (though certainly brisk) waters of Herring Cove Beach. Though technically illegal, nude sunbathers head left to the south section of the beach; families usually break out the picnic baskets closer to the parking lot. The entire beach faces west, making it a spectacular place to be at sunset.

MELISSAMN/SHUTTERSTOCK ©

Three Sisters Lights

While visiting Nauset Light Beach, don't miss this curious trio of 19th-century lighthouses (Cable Rd) – they were saved from an eroding sea cliff and moved to a wooded clearing just five minutes' walk up Cable Rd from Nauset Light.

Nauset Light

Nauset Light (www.nausetlight.org) is a picturesque red-and-white lighthouse guarding the shoreline at the Nauset Light Beach. Look familiar? You may have seen it on all the Cape Cod potato-chip packets! It's open to the public for free tours Sundays from May to October and on Tuesdays and Wednesdays in June through August.

MIRCEA COSTINA/SHUTTERSTOCK ©

Fort Hill

Don't miss the commanding view of expansive Nauset Marsh from Fort Hill. It's a favorite place to be at dawn, but the view is memorable any time of the day. And bring your walking shoes for the 2-mile Fort Hill Trail. It leads down scenic Fort Hill toward the coast and then skirts inland to meander along raised boardwalks over a unique red-maple swamp. It's one of the nicest walks in the National Seashore, especially in fall.

NAVADADARA/SHUTTERSTOCK ©

LUCKY-PHOTOGRAPHER/SHUTTERSTOCK ©

Race Point Beach

On the wild tip of the Cape, Race Point Beach is a breathtaking stretch of sand, crashing surf and undulating dunes as far as the eye can see. Kick off your sandals, kids – the soft, grainy sand makes for a fun run. This is the kind of beach where you could walk for miles and see no one but the occasional angler casting for bluefish.

CINDY GOFF/SHUTTERSTOCK ©

Head of the Meadow Beach

Wide, dune-backed Head of the Meadow Beach has limited facilities, but there are lifeguards in summer. If you happen to be there at low tide, you might catch a glimpse of old shipwrecks that met their fate on the shoals. There are two entrances: the National Seashore beach (parking $20) is to the left and open to the public. The other entrance is for local residents only.

Province Lands Bike Trail

Province Lands Bike Trail (www.nps.gov/thingstodo/bike-the-province-lands-bike-trail.htm) is an exhilarating 7.5 miles of paved bike trails crisscrossing the forest and undulating dunes of the Cape Cod National Seashore. As a bonus, you can cool off with a swim: the main 5.5-mile loop trail has spur trails leading to Herring Cove Beach and Race Point Beach.

Stonewall National Monument

In 2016 President Barack Obama declared Christopher Park, a small fenced-in triangle with benches and some greenery in the heart of the West Village, a **national park** (www. nps.gov/ston; W 4th St, btwn Christopher & Grove Sts, West Village) and on it the first national monument dedicated to LGBTIQ+ history. It's well worth stopping here to reflect on the Stonewall uprising of 1969, when LGBTIQ+ citizens fought back against discriminatory policing of their communities – many consider the event the birth of the modern LGBTIQ+ rights movement in the US.

National Parks of New York Harbor

There are 11 sites managed by the National Park Service surrounding the port of New York City, preserving more than 400 years of American history.

Gateway National Recreation Area

Consisting of several, disparate geographic 'units' totaling 27,000 National Park Service–run acres, Gateway (www.nps.gov/gate) is possibly most well known for its Sandy Hook and New Jersey beaches, and Jamaica Bay's wetlands for bird-watching. Lesser visited spots include Floyd Bennett Field near Rockaway, Queens, and Canarsie Pier in Brooklyn.

African Burial Ground National Monument

In 1991, construction workers at this **site** (www.nps.gov/afbg; 290 Broadway, btwn Duane & Reade Sts, Lower Manhattan) uncovered more than 400 stacked wooden caskets, just 16ft to 28ft below street level. The boxes contained the remains of both enslaved and free African Americans from the 17th and 18th centuries (from 1697, nearby Trinity Church refused them burial in its graveyard). Today, a poignant memorial site and a visitor center with four rooms of educational displays honor the estimated 15,000 men, women and children buried in America's largest and oldest African cemetery.

Theodore Roosevelt Birthplace

Learn about the 26th president's extraordinary life, which has been somewhat overshadowed by the enduring legacy of his younger cousin Franklin D, at this **national historic site** (www.nps.gov/thrb; 28 E 20th St, btwn Broadway & Park Ave S, Flatiron District). It's a bit of a cheat, since the physical house where the 26th president was actually born was demolished in his own lifetime, but this building is a worthy reconstruction by his relatives, who took painstaking steps to bring together original furniture from the residence with true-to-the-period restorations.

Hamilton Grange National Memorial

This Federal-style **retreat** (www.nps.gov/hagr; St Nicholas Park, at 141st St) belonged to Founding Father Alexander Hamilton, who owned a 32-acre country estate here in the early 1800s. Unfortunately, Hamilton was able to enjoy his abode for only two years before his life was cut short in a fatal duel with political rival Aaron Burr. Moved from Convent Ave to its present location in 2008, the building is one of several Hamilton-related sights seeing an increase in visitors – by some 75% – thanks to Lin-Manuel Miranda's musical, *Hamilton*.

Statue of Liberty & Ellis Island

Since her unveiling in 1886, Lady Liberty (ww.nps.gov/stli) has symbolized hope for millions of immigrants sailing into New York Harbor in search of a better life. The statue now welcomes millions of tourists, many of whom head up to her crown for one of New York City's finest skyline and water views. Close by lies Ellis Island (www.nps.gov/elis), the American gateway for over 12 million new arrivals between 1892 and 1954. These days it's home to one of the city's most moving museums, paying tribute to these immigrants and their indelible courage.

Book tickets online and, if you can, catch an early ferry and avoid weekends, especially in summer. You'll need a good four or five hours to explore the two sights properly, and you'll want to bring a picnic lunch.

Below: Statue of Liberty; Below left and right: Ellis Island National Museum of Immigration

Governors Island National Monument

Off-limits to the public for 200 years, former military outpost Governors Island (www.govisland. com) is now one of New York's most popular seasonal playgrounds. The fort-studded island is seven minutes by ferry from Manhattan, and threaded with cycling and walking trails. Playgrounds and picnic areas look across the water to views of glinting skyscrapers. With the city din of heli- copters and distant traffic, you won't forget you're in NYC – but it's an invigorating interlude with historic sites to explore.

National Park Service rangers conduct guided tours of the historic district (see www.nps.gov/gois for specific days and times) including star-shaped **Fort Jay**, built in 1794 and rebuilt 15 years later, a failed attempt to prevent the British from invading Manhattan; **Colonels Row**, a collection of 19th-century brick officers' quarters; and the red sandstone **Castle Williams**, a 19th-century fort that was later converted to a military penitentiary.

Liggett Terrace hosts food trucks and an outpost of Brooklyn beer favorite Threes Brewing; there's the biggest choice of refreshments on weekends. **Hammock Grove** has 50 hammocks to relax in, along with lawns and kids' play areas.

The Hills, in the southwest part of the island, have flower-fringed walking trails up to panoramic views of Manhattan (from 70ft high), while the **Great Promenade**, running for 2.2 miles along the island's perimeter, takes in everything from Lower Manhattan and Brooklyn to Staten Island and New Jersey.

Below: Manhattan from Governors Island; Below left: Liggett Hall; Below right: Castle Williams

KAZ7/SHUTTERSTOCK ©

LEONARD ZHUKOVSKY/SHUTTERSTOCK ©

PISAPHOTOGRAPHY/SHUTTERSTOCK ©

ROB U/SSELSTEIN/SHUTTERSTOCK ©

Skyline Drive

Shenandoah National Park

Shenandoah is a showcase of natural color and beauty: in spring and summer the wildflowers explode, in fall the leaves burn red and orange, and in winter a starkly beautiful hibernation period sets in. White-tailed deer are common and, with luck, you might spot a black bear, bobcat or wild turkey.

Great For...

State
Virginia

Entrance Fee
7-day pass per car/motorcycle/person on foot or bicycle $30/25/15

Area
310 sq miles

With the famous 105-mile Skyline Dr and more than 500 miles of hiking trails, including 101 miles of the Appalachian Trail, there is plenty to do and see.

Skyline Drive

A 105-mile-long road running down the spine of the Blue Ridge Mountains, Shenandoah National Park's Skyline Dr (p66) redefines the definition of 'Scenic Route.' You're constantly treated to an impressive view, but keep in mind the road is bendy and slow-going (35mph limit), and is congested in peak season.

It's best to start this drive just south of Front Royal, VA; from here you'll snake over Virginia wine and hill country. Numbered mileposts mark the way; there are lots of pull-offs. Our favorite is around Mile 51.2, where you can take a moderately difficult 3.6-mile-loop hike to **Lewis Spring Falls**.

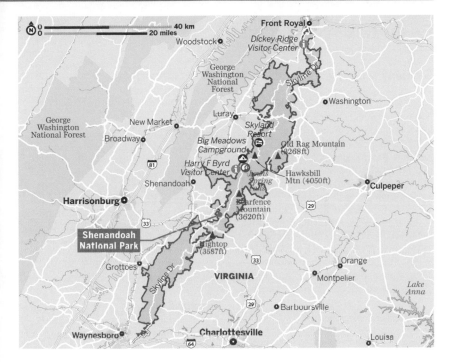

Hiking

The hike to the rocky summit of **Old Rag Mountain** is one of the best in the state. This extremely tough, full-day 9.2-mile circuit trail culminates in an adventurous rocky scramble – one that's suitable only for the physically fit. Your reward is the summit of Old Rag Mountain, not to mention the fantastic views along the way.

Hawksbill Summit is another breathtaking hiking destination (literally). The tremendous climb to the park's highest peak offers an unforgettable picture of the mountain landscape. There are two options: either a 2.9-mile loop or 1.7-mile up-and-back. For the shorter route, start at the Hawksbill Gap parking area (Mile 45.6) and look for the Lower Hawksbill Trail, which leads into the woods. The steep ascent is lined with mountain ash and red spruce – beware of small, frequent rockslides along the jumbled path.

At **Bearfence Mountain** a short trail leads to a spectacular 360-degree viewpoint. The circuit hike is only 1.2 miles, but one section involves an adventurous scramble over rocks.

Cycling

The park holds occasional 'Ride the Drive' car-free days when Skyline Dr is closed to motorized vehicles from Mile 0 south to Mile 31.5 in the northern district, leaving it open for cyclists. Check the park website to see when the next car-free day is scheduled.

Essential Information

Sleeping & Eating

The park has two lodges, five campgrounds, a number of rental cabins and free backcountry camping. Camping is at five National Park Service (NPS) campgrounds; four cater to individuals, one is for larger groups only. Most are open from mid-May to October. Camping elsewhere requires a backcountry permit, available for free from any visitor center.

Skyland and Big Meadows both have restaurants, plus taverns with occasional live music. You can buy boxed lunches at Big Meadows Lodge and to-go sandwiches in the Skyland lobby area and near the camp store at Big Meadows. If you're going camping or on extended hikes, it's best to bring your own food into the park.

Big Meadows Campground (☎877-444-6777; www.recreation.gov; Mile 51.3, Skyline Dr; tent & RV sites $20; ☺May-Oct) Find the perfect spot among 217 nonelectric sites and you might just snap a quick photo of a resident bear lumbering past your campfire. This campground tends to be crowded, especially during fall, but it's smack in the middle of Skyline Dr, has good facilities (flush toilets, showers, store, laundry) and is a convenient base for all exploration.

Skyland Resort (☎855-470-6005; www.goshenandoah.com; Mile 41.7, Skyline Dr; r $141-265, cabins $130-281; ☺late Mar–mid-Nov; ❄☎) Founded in 1888, this spectacularly located resort commands views over the countryside. You'll find a variety of room types, including renovated premium rooms; rustic but comfy cabins; a taproom with a live entertain-ment program; and a full-service dining room. You can also arrange horseback rides from here. Opens a month or so before Big Meadows in the spring.

Spottswood Dining Room (www.visitshenan doah.com; Mile 51.3, Skyline Dr, Big Meadows Lodge; lunch mains $8-17, dinner mains $12-28; ☺7:30-10am, noon-2pm & 5:30-9pm early May-early Nov) The wide-ranging menu at the dining room in Big Meadows Lodge makes the most of locally sourced ingredients. Complement your food with Virginian wines and local microbrews, all enjoyed in an old-fashioned rustic-lodge ambience. There's also a taproom (2pm to 11pm) with a limited menu and live entertainment.

Visitor Centers

There are two visitor centers in the park. Both have maps and backcountry permits, as well as information about outdoor activities.

Dickey Ridge (www.nps.gov/shen; Mile 4.6, Skyline Dr; ☺9am-5pm Mon-Fri, to 6pm Sat & Sun, closed late Nov-early Apr) In the north.

Harry F Byrd (www.nps.gov/shen; Mile 51, Skyline Dr; ☺9am-5pm late Mar-late Nov, 9:30am-4pm Fri-Sun late Nov-late Mar) In the south.

Getting There & Around

The park lies just 75 miles west of Washington, DC, and can be easily accessed from several exits off I-81.

Top left: Blue Ridge; Top right: On Bearfence Mountain; Bottom: Old Rag Mountain

CLASSIC ROAD TRIPS

Skyline Drive

The centerpiece of the ribbon-thin Shenandoah National Park is the jaw-dropping beauty of Skyline Drive, which runs for just over 100 miles atop the Blue Ridge Mountains. Unlike the massive acreage of western parks like Yellowstone or Yosemite, Shenandoah is at times only a mile wide. That may seem to narrow the park's scope, yet it makes it a perfect space for traversing and road-tripping goodness.

Distance 150 miles

Duration 3 days

Best Time to Go
May to November for great weather, open facilities and clear views.

Essential Photo
The fabulous 360-degree horizon at the top of Bearfence Mountain.

Best for Culture
Byrd Visitor Center offers an illuminating peek into Appalachian folkways.

❶ Front Royal
Straddling the northern entrance to the park is the tiny city of Front Royal. Although it's not among Virginia's fanciest ports of call, this lush riverside town offers all the urban amenities you might need before a camping or hiking trip up in the mountains.

If you need to gather your bearings, an obvious place to start is the **Front Royal**

Visitor Center (📞540-635 5788, 800-338-2576; www.discoverfrontroyal.com; 414 E Main St; ⏱9am-5pm, closed Tue). Friendly staff are on hand to overwhelm you with information about what to do in the area.

The Drive ≫ Dinosaur Land is 10 miles north of Front Royal, towards Winchester, via US 340 (Stonewall Jackson Hwy).

❷ Dinosaur Land
Before you head into the national park and its stunning natural beauty, visit **Dinosaur Land** (📞540-869-2222; www.dinosaurland. com; 3848 Stonewall Jackson Hwy, White Post; adult/child 2-10yr $8/6; ⏱9:30am-5:30pm Mar-May, to 6pm Jun-Aug, to 5pm Sep-Dec; 🚻) for some fantastic artificial tackiness. This spectacularly low-brow shrine to concrete sculpture is not to be missed. Although it's an 'educational prehistoric forest,' with more than 50 life-size dinosaurs (and a King Kong for good measure), you'd probably learn more about the tenants by fast-forwarding through *Jurassic Park 3*. But that's not why you've stopped here, so grab your camera and sidle up to the triceratops for memories that will last a millennium.

The Drive ≫ Head back to Front Royal, then go south on US 522 (Remount Rd) for about 9 miles to reach Huntly.

❸ Huntly
Huntly is a small-ish town nestled in the green foothills of the Shenandoahs, lying just in the southern shadows of Front Royal. It's a good spot to refuel on some cosmopolitan culture and foodie deliciousness in the form of **Rappahannock Cellars** (📞540-635-9398; www.rappahannockcellars. com; 14437 Hume Rd; wine/sprits tasting $10/12; ⏱noon-6pm), one of the nicer wineries of north-central Virginia, where vineyard-covered hills shadow the horizon, like some slice of northern Italian pastoral prettiness that got lost somewhere in the upcountry of the Old Dominion. Give the port a whirl (well, maybe not if you're driving).

The Drive » Head back to Front Royal, as you'll enter Skyline Drive from there. From the beginning of Skyline Drive, it's 5.5 miles to Dickey Ridge.

❹ Skyline Drive: The Beginning

Skyline Drive is the scenic drive to end all scenic drives. The 75 overlooks, with views into the Shenandoah Valley and the Piedmont, are all breathtaking. In spring and summer, endless variations on the color green are sure to enchant, just as the vibrant reds and yellows will amaze you in autumn. This might be your chance to finally hike a section of the Appalachian Trail, which crosses Skyline Drive in 32 places.

The logical first stop on an exploration of Skyline Drive and Shenandoah National Park is the **Dickey Ridge Visitor Center** (www.nps.gov/shen; Mile 4.6, Skyline Dr; ⊘9am-5pm Apr-Nov). It's not just an informative leaping-off point; it's a building with a fascinating history all of its own. This spot

originally operated as a 'wild' dining hall in 1908 (back then that simply meant it had a terrace for dancing). However, it closed during WWII and didn't reopen until 1958, when it became a visitor center. Now it's one of the park's two main information centers and contains a little bit of everything you'll need to get started on your trip along Skyline Drive.

The Drive » It's a twisty 19 more miles along Skyline Drive to Mathews Arm.

❺ Mathews Arm & Elkwallow

Mathews Arm is the first major section of Shenandoah National Park you encounter after leaving Dickey Ridge. Before you get there, you can stop at a pullover at Mile 19.4 and embark on a 4.8-mile loop hike to **Little Devils Stairs**. Getting through this narrow gorge is as tough as the name suggests; expect hand-over-hand climbing for some portions.

At Mathews Arm there's a campground as well as an amphitheater, and some

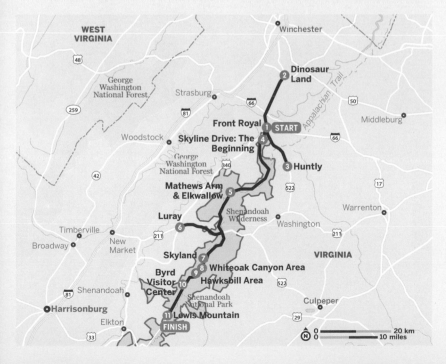

nice breezes; early on in your drive, you're already at a 2750ft altitude.

From the amphitheater, it's a 6.5-mile moderately taxing hike to lovely **Overall Run Falls**, the tallest in the national park (93ft). There are plenty of rock ledges where you can enjoy the view and snap a picture, but be warned that the falls sometimes dry out in the summer. **Elkwallow Wayside**, which includes a nice picnic area and lookout, is at Mile 24, just past Mathews Arm.

The Drive » From Mathews Arm, proceed south along Skyline Drive for about 10 miles, then take the US 211 ramp westbound for about 7 miles to reach Luray.

❻ Luray

Luray is a good spot to grab some grub and potentially rest your head if you're not into camping. It's also where you'll find the wonderful **Luray Caverns** (☑540-743-6551; www.

luraycaverns.com; 101 Cave Hill Rd; adult/child 6-12yr $30/15; ⏲9am-7pm mid-Jun–Aug, to 6pm Sep-Nov & Apr–mid-Jun, to 4pm Mon-Fri, to 5pm Sat & Sun Dec-Mar), one of the most extensive cavern systems on the East Coast.

Here you can take a one-hour, roughly 1-mile guided tour of the caves, opened to the public more than 100 years ago. The rock formations throughout are quite stunning, and Luray boasts what is surely a one-of-a-kind attraction – the Stalacpipe Organ – in the pit of its belly. This crazy contraption has been banging out melodies on the rock formations for decades. As the guide says, the caves are 400 million years old '*if* you believe in geological dating' (if the subtext is lost on you, understand this is a conservative part of the country where Creationism is widely accepted, if hotly debated). No matter what you believe in, you'll be impressed by the fantastic underground expanses.

Below: Bearfence Mountain; Below left: Front Royal; Below right: Overall Run Falls

Next to the Luray Caverns is an excellent opportunity to let your inner Shelley Duvall or Scatman Crothers run wild. Go screaming *The Shining*–style through the **Garden Maze**, but beware! This maze is harder than it looks and some could spend longer inside it than they anticipated. Paranormal and psychic abilities are permitted, but frowned upon, when solving the hedge maze. Redrum! Redrum!

The Drive » Take US 211 east for 10 miles to get back on Skyline Drive. Then proceed 10 miles south along Skyline Drive to get to Skyland. Along the way you'll drive over the highest point of Skyline Drive (3680ft). At Mile 40.5, just before reaching Skyland, you can enjoy amazing views from the parking overlook at Thorofare Mountain (3595ft).

❼ Skyland

Horse-fanciers will want to book a trail ride through Shenandoah at **Skyland Stables** (📞877-847-1919; www.goshenandoah.com; Mile 42.5, Skyline Dr; guided group rides 1/2½hr $50/110; ⏰9am-5pm Mon-Thu, from 8am Fri-Sun Apr–mid-Nov). Rides last up to 2½ hours and are a great way to see the wildlife and epic vistas. Pony rides are also available for the wee members of your party. This is a good spot to break up your trip if you're into hiking (and if you're on this trip, we're assuming you are).

You've got great access to local trailheads around here, and the sunsets are fabulous. The accommodations are a little rustic, but in a charming way (the Trout Cabin was built in 1911 and it feels like it, but we mean this in the most complimentary way possible). The place positively oozes nostalgia, but if you're into amenities, you may find it a little dilapidated.

The Drive » It's only 1.5 miles south on Skyline Drive to get to the Whiteoak parking area.

❽ Whiteoak Canyon Area

At Mile 42.6, Whiteoak Canyon is another area of Skyline Drive that offers unmatched hiking and exploration opportunities.

There are several parking areas that all provide different entry points to the various trails that snake through this ridge- and stream-scape.

Most hikers are attracted to Whiteoak Canyon for its **waterfalls** – there are six in total, with the tallest topping out at 86ft high. At the Whiteoak parking area, you can make a 4.6-mile round-trip hike to these cascades, but beware – it's both a steep climb up and back to your car. To reach the next set of waterfalls, you'll have to add 2.7 miles to the round trip and prepare yourself for a steep (1100ft) elevation shift.

The **Limberlost Trail** and parking area is just south of Whiteoak Canyon. This is a moderately difficult 1.3-mile trek into spruce upcountry thick with hawks, owls and other birds; the boggy ground is home to many salamanders.

The Drive » It's about 3 miles south of Whiteoak Canyon to the Hawksbill area via Skyline Drive.

❾ Hawksbill Area

Once you reach Mile 45.6, you've reached Hawksbill, the name of both this part of Skyline Drive and the tallest peak in Shenandoah National Park. Numerous trails in this area skirt the summits of the mountain.

Pull into the parking area at Hawksbill Gap (Mile 45.6). You've got a few hiking options to pick from. The **Lower Hawksbill Trail** is a steep 1.7-mile round trip that circles Hawksbill's lower slopes. The huff-inducing ascent yields a pretty great view over the park. Another great lookout lies at the end of the **Upper Hawksbill Trail**, a moderately difficult 2.1-mile trip. You can link up with the Appalachian Trail here via a spur called the Salamander Trail.

If you continue south for about 5 miles you'll reach **Fishers Gap Overlook**. The attraction here is the **Rose River Loop**, a 4-mile, moderately strenuous trail that is positively Edenic. Along the way you'll pass by waterfalls, under thick forest canopy and over swift-running streams.

The Drive »From Fishers Gap, head about a mile south to the Byrd Visitor Center, technically located at Mile 51.

⑩ Byrd Visitor Center

The **Harry F Byrd Visitor Center** (www. nps.gov/shen; Mile 51, Skyline Dr; ⊙9am-5pm Apr-Nov) is the central visitor center of Shenandoah National Park, marking (roughly) a halfway point between the two ends of Skyline Drive. It's devoted to explaining the settlement and development of Shenandoah Valley via a series of small but well-curated exhibitions; as such, it's a good place to stop and learn about the surrounding culture (and pick up backcountry camping permits). There are camping and ranger activities in the **Big Meadows** area, located across the road from the visitor center.

The **Story of the Forest** trail is an easy, paved, 1.8-mile loop that's quite pretty; the trailhead connects to the visitor center. You can also explore two nearby waterfalls. **Dark Hollow Falls**, which sounds (and looks) like something out of a Tolkien novel, is a 70ft-high cascade located at the end of a quite steep 1.4-mile trail. **Lewis Falls**,

accessed via Big Meadows, is on a moderately difficult 3.3-mile trail that intersects the Appalachian Trail; at one point you'll be scrabbling up a rocky slope.

The Drive »The Lewis Mountain area is about 5 miles south of the Byrd Visitor Center via Skyline Drive. Stop for good overlooks at Milam Gap and Naked Creek (both clearly signposted from the road).

⑪ Lewis Mountain

Lewis Mountain is both the name of one of the major camping areas of Shenandoah National Park and a nearby 3570ft mountain. The trail to the mountain is only about a mile long with a small elevation gain, and leads to a nice overlook. But the best view here is at the **Bearfence Rock Scramble.** That name is no joke; this 1.2-mile hike gets steep and rocky, and you don't want to attempt it during or after rainfall. The reward is one of the best panoramas of the Shenandoahs. After you leave, remember there's still about 50 miles of Skyline Drive between you and the park exit at Rockfish Gap.

Luray Caverns

CLASSIC ROAD TRIPS

The Civil War Tour

The Civil War was fought from 1861 to 1865 in the nation's backyards, many of which are between Washington, DC, and Richmond, VA. On this trip you'll cross battlefields where more than 100,000 Americans perished and are buried, foe beside foe; many of these are now preserved by the National Park Service. Amid rolling farmlands, sunny hills and deep forests, you'll discover a jarring juxtaposition of bloody legacy and bucolic scenery, and along the way, the places where America forged its identity.

Distance 320 miles

Duration 3 days

Best Time to Go
September to November; the brisk air still comes with sunny skies, and autumnal color shows at preserved battlefields.

Essential Photo
The fences and fields of Antietam at sunset.

Best for Foodies
Lamb burger at Burger Bach.

❶ Antietam
While the majority of this trip takes place in Virginia, there is ground to be covered in neighboring Maryland, a border state officially allied with the Union yet close enough to the South to possess Southern sympathies. Confederate general Robert E Lee, hoping to capitalize on a friendly populace, tried to invade Maryland early in the conflict.

The subsequent Battle of Antietam, fought in Sharpsburg, MD, on September 17, 1862, has the dubious distinction of marking the bloodiest day in American history. The site is preserved at **Antietam National Battlefield** (📞301-432-5124; www.nps.gov/anti; 5831 Dunker Church Rd, Sharpsburg; 3-day pass per person/vehicle $7/15; ⊗grounds sunrise-sunset, visitor center 9am-5pm) in the corn-and-hill country of north-central Maryland.

As befits an engagement that claimed 22,000 casualties in the course of a single, nightmarish day, even the local geographic nomenclature became violent. An area known as Sunken Rd turned into 'Bloody Lane' after bodies were stacked there. In the park's cemetery, many Union gravestones bear the names of Irish and German immigrants who died in a country they had only recently adopted.

The Drive » Take MD 65 south out of Antietam to Sharpsburg, then take MD 34 east for 6 miles, then turn right onto US 40A (eastbound). Take this for 11 miles, then merge onto US 70 south, followed 3 miles later by US 270 (bypassing Frederick). Take 270 south to the Beltway (I-495); access exit 45B to get to I-66 east, eventually leading to the National Mall.

❷ Washington, DC
Washington, DC, was the capital of the Union during the Civil War, just as it is the capital of the country today. While the city was never invaded by the Confederacy, thousands of Union soldiers passed through, trained and drilled inside the city; indeed, the official name of the North's main fighting force was the Army of the Potomac.

The **National Museum of American History** (📞202-633-1000; www.american history.si.edu; 1300 Constitution Ave NW, btwn 12th and 14th Sts NW; ⊗10am-5:30pm, to 7:30pm some days; ♿) **FREE**, located directly on the **National Mall**, has good permanent

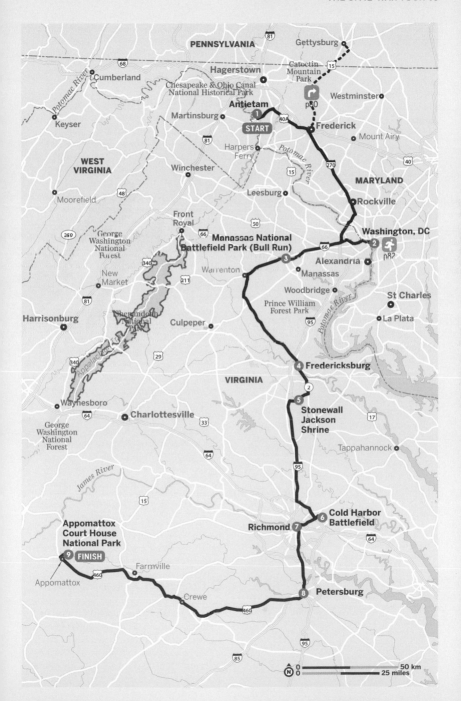

exhibitions on the Civil War. Perhaps more importantly, it provides visitors with the context for understanding why the war happened.

Following the war, a grateful nation erected many monuments to Union generals. A statue worth visiting is the **African American Civil War Memorial** (www. afroamcivilwar.org; cnr U St NW & Vermont Ave NW, U Street; ⏱24hr), next to the eastern exit of the U St Metro stop, inscribed with the names of soldiers of color who served in the Union army.

The Drive » From Washington, DC, it takes about an hour driving along I-66W through the tangled knots of suburban sprawl that blanket Northern Virginia to reach Manassas.

❸ Manassas National Battlefield (Bull Run)

The site of the first major pitched battle of the Civil War is mere minutes from the strip malls of Northern Virginia. NPS-run **Manassas National Battlefield Park** (☎703-361-1339; www.nps.gov/mana; 6511 Sudley Rd, off I-66; ⏱park dawn-dusk, visitor center 8:30am-5pm) **FREE** occupies the site where, in 1861, 35,000 Union soldiers and 32,500 Confederates saw the same view you have today – a stretch of gorgeous countryside that has miraculously survived the predations of the army of Northern Virginia real estate developers.

This is as close as many will come to 19th-century rural America; distant hills, dark, brooding tree lines, low curving fields and the soft hump of overgrown trench works.

Following the battle, both sides realized a long war was at hand. Europe watched nervously; in a matter of weeks, the world's largest army was the Union Army of the Potomac. The second biggest was the Confederate States Army. A year later, at the Battle of Shiloh, 24,000 men were listed as casualties – more than all the accumulated casualties of every previous American war.

The Drive » In Manassas, take US 29N for 13 miles and then turn left onto US 17S (Marsh Rd). Follow 17/Marsh Rd south for about 35 miles to get to downtown Fredericksburg.

❹ Fredericksburg

If battlefields preserve rural, agricultural America, Fredericksburg is an example of what the nation's main streets once looked like – orderly grids, touches of green and friendly storefronts. But for all its cuteness, this is the site of one of the worst blunders in American military history. In 1862, when the Northern Army attempted a massed charge against an entrenched Confederate position, a Southern artilleryman looked at the bare slope Union forces had to cross and told a commanding officer, 'A chicken could not live on that field when we open on it.' Sixteen charges resulted in an estimated 6000 to 8000 Union casualties.

Fredericksburg & Spotsylvania National Military Park (☎540-693-3200; www.nps.gov/frsp; 1013 Lafayette Blvd; ⏱Fredericksburg & Chancellorsville visitor centers 9am-5pm, hours vary at other exhibit areas) **FREE** is not as immediately compelling as Manassas because of the thick forest that still covers the battlefields, but the woods themselves are a sylvan wonder. Again, the pretty nature of...well, nature, grows over graves; the nearby Battle of the Wilderness was named for these thick woods, which caught fire and killed hundreds of wounded soldiers after the shooting was finished.

The Drive » From Fredericksburg, take US 17 south for 5 miles, after which 77 becomes VA 2 (also known as Sandy Lane Dr and Fredericksburg Turnpike). Follow this road for 5 more miles, then turn right onto Stonewall Jackson Rd (State Rd 606).

❺ Stonewall Jackson Shrine

In Chancellorsville, Robert E Lee, outnumbered two to one, split his forces and attacked both flanks of the Union army. The audacity of the move caused the Northern force to crumble and flee across the Potomac, but the victory was a costly one;

Below: Manassas National Battlefield; Below left: Antietam National Battlefield; Below right: Fredericksburg & Spotsylvania National Military Park

in the course of the fighting, Lee's ablest general, Stonewall Jackson, had his arm shot off by a nervous Confederate sentry. The arm is buried at nearby **Ellwood Manor** (540-786-2880; www.fowb.org; 36380 Constitution Hwy, Rte 20, Locust Grove; 10am-5pm early Jun-Aug, Sat & Sun only Apr-early Jun & Aug-Nov) FREE . Ask a ranger for directions.

The wound was patched, but Jackson went on to contract a fatal dose of pneumonia. He was taken to what is now called the **Stonewall Jackson Shrine** (804-633-6076; www.nps.gov/frsp; 12019 Stonewall Jackson Rd, Woodford; grounds sunrise-sunset, building 9am-5pm) FREE in nearby Guinea Station. In a small white cabin set against attractive Virginia horse-country, overrun with sprays of purple flowers and daisy fields, Jackson uttered a series of prolonged ramblings. He fell silent, then whispered, 'Let us cross over the river and rest in the shade of the trees,' and died.

The Drive » You can get here via I-95, which you take to I-295S (then take exit 34A), which takes 50 minutes. Or, for a back road experience (one hour, 10 minutes), take VA 2S south for 35 miles until it connects to VA 643/Rural Point Rd. Stay on VA 643 until it becomes VA 156/Cold Harbor Rd, which leads to the battlefield.

❻ Cold Harbor Battlefield

By 1864, Union general Ulysses Grant was ready to take the battle into Virginia. His subsequent invasion, dubbed the Overland (or Wilderness) Campaign, was one of the bloodiest of the war. It reached a violent climax at Cold Harbor, just north of Richmond.

At the site now known as **Cold Harbor Battlefield** (804-226-1981; www.nps.gov; 5515 Anderson-Wright Dr, Mechanicsville; sunrise-sunset, visitor center 9am-4:30pm) FREE , Grant threw his men into a full-frontal assault; the resultant casualties were horrendous, and a precursor to WWI trench warfare.

The area has now reverted to a forest and field checkerboard overseen by the National Park Service. Ask a local ranger to direct you to the **Third Turnout**, a series of Union earthworks from where you can look out at the most preserved section of the fight: the long, low field that Northern soldiers charged across. This landscape has essentially not changed in more than 150 years.

The Drive » From Cold Harbor, head north on VA 156/Cold Harbor Rd for about 3 miles until it intersects Creighton Rd. Turn left on Creighton and follow it for 6 miles into downtown Richmond.

❼ Richmond

There are two Civil War museums in the former capitol of the Confederacy, and they make for an interesting study in contrasts. Both are now managed by the American Civil War Center. The first is the **Museum of the Confederacy (MOC)**, which was once a shrine to the Southern 'Lost Cause,' and still attracts some neo-Confederate types. But the MOC has also graduated into a respected educational institution, and its collection of Confederate artifacts is probably the best in the country. The optional tour of the **Confederate White House** is recommended for its quirky insights (did you know the second-most powerful man in the Confederacy may have been a gay Jew?).

The second **museum** (804-649-1861; https://acwm.org; 500 Tredegar St, Gambles Hill; adult/child 6-17yr $15/8; 9am-5pm), inside the old Tredegar ironworks (the main armament producer for the Confederacy), makes an admirable, ultimately successful, effort to present the war from three perspectives: Northern, Southern and African American. The permanent exhibits are well presented, the rotating exhibits insightful. The effect is clearly powerful and occasionally divisive, a testament to the conflict's lasting impact.

The Drive » Take Rte 95 southbound for about 23 miles and get on exit 52. Get onto 301 (Wythe St) and follow until it becomes Washington St, and eventually VA 35/Oaklawn Dr. Look for signs to the battlefield park from here.

❽ Petersburg

Petersburg, just south of Richmond, is the blue-collar sibling city to the Virginia capital, its center gutted by white flight following desegregation. **Petersburg National Battlefield Park** (☏804-732-3531; www.nps.gov/pete; 5001 Siege Rd, Eastern Front Visitor Center; ⏰visitor center 9am-5pm, grounds 8:30am-dusk) **FREE** marks the spot where Northern and Southern soldiers spent almost a quarter of the war in a protracted, entrenched standoff. The Battle of the Crater, famously depicted in Charles Frazier's novel *Cold Mountain,* was an attempt by Union soldiers to break this stalemate by tunneling under the Confederate lines and blowing up their fortifications. After the explosion, Union soldiers rushed into the newly formed crater, where they became easy targets for uninjured Confederate troops, who shot them down like fish in a barrel.

The Drive » Drive south of Petersburg, then west through a skein of back roads to follow Lee's last retreat. Another option is to take VA 460 west from Petersburg, then connect to VA 635, which leads to Appomattox via VA 24, near Farmville.

❾ Appomattox Court House National Park

About 92 miles west of Petersburg is **Appomattox Court House National Park** (☏434-352-8987; www.nps.gov/apco; 111 National Park Dr; ⏰9am-5pm) **FREE**, where the Confederacy finally surrendered. The park itself is wide and lovely, and the ranger staff are extremely helpful.

There are several **marker stones** dedicated to the surrendering Confederates; the most touching one marks the spot where Robert E Lee rode back from Appomattox after surrendering to Union general Ulysses Grant. Lee's soldiers stood on either side of the field waiting for the return of their commander. When Lee rode into sight, he doffed his hat; the troops surged toward him, some saying goodbye while others, too overcome with emotion to speak, passed their hands over the white flanks of Lee's horse, Traveller. It's a spot that's dedicated to defeat, humility and reconciliation; the imperfect realization of all those qualities is the character of the America you've been driving through.

Appomattox Court House

Civil War Sites

The Civil War began in April 1861, when the Confederacy attacked Fort Sumter in Charleston, SC, and raged on for the next four years. By the end, as many as 750,000 soldiers, nearly an entire generation of young men, were dead; Southern plantations and cities (most notably Atlanta) lay sacked and burned. Hundreds of structures and sites affected by or built in commemoration of the Civil War are preserved and managed by the National Park Service today.

Monocacy National Battlefield

The crucial but little known Battle of Monocacy (www.nps.gov/mono) occurred during the last Confederate invasion of the North, which began when Confederate general Jubal Early pushed toward Washington, DC, with 15,000 troops. A Union force of 6600, led by General Lew Wallace, clashed with the rebels here on July 9, 1864, delaying their march by one day. This delay gave Union reinforcements time to organize, ultimately saving the nation's capital. Hiking trails and a driving tour stop by key battle sights.

Harriet Tubman Underground Railroad National Historic Park

Maryland's newest national historic park (www.nps.gov/hatu) preserves sights connected with the Underground Railroad's most famous conductor, who helped transport nearly 70 enslaved people to new lives of freedom. Harriet Tubman was born on nearby Greenbrier Rd. The visitor center is a helpful orientation point for exploring the Harriet Tubman Underground Railroad Byway, which stops here and at 35 other related sites on the Eastern Shore. It's co-managed by the National Park Service and Maryland state parks.

WIRESTOCK, INC./ALAMY STOCK PHOTO ©

Contrabands & Freedmen Cemetery Memorial

During the Civil War, the Union-controlled Southern city of Alexandria, VA, became a safe haven for formerly enslaved African Americans. Some 1800 contrabands (as freed slaves were called) and freedmen were buried at this cemetery (www.alexandriava.gov/FreedmenMemorial) on Alexandria's southern edge. A memorial park was developed on the site, including the sculpture, *The Path of Thorns and Roses*, symbolizing the freedom struggle.

JAMES KIRKIKIS/SHUTTERSTOCK ©

Fort Warren

Georges Island, in the Boston Harbor Islands National Recreation Area, is the site of Fort Warren, a 19th-century fort and Civil War prison. National Park Service rangers give guided tours of the fort, with its many dark tunnels, creepy corners and magnificent lookouts.

Gettysburg National Military Park

The Battle of Gettysburg, fought in Gettysburg, PA, in July of 1863, marked the turning point of the war and the high-water mark of the Confederacy's attempted rebellion. Lee never made a gambit as bold as this invasion of the North, and his army (arguably) never recovered from the defeat it suffered here.

Gettysburg National Military Park (www.nps.gov/gett), one hour and 40 minutes north of DC, does an excellent job of explaining the course and context of the combat. Look for **Little Round Top Hill**, where a Union unit checked a Southern flanking maneuver, and the field of **Pickett's Charge**, where the Confederacy suffered its most crushing defeat up to that point. Following the battle, Abraham Lincoln gave his Gettysburg Address here to mark the victory and the 'new birth of the nation' on the country's birthday: July 4.

You can easily lose a day here just soaking up the scenery – a gorgeous swath of rolling hills and lush forest interspersed with hollows, rock formations and patches of farmland. To get here, jump on US 15 northbound for about 45 miles.

DELMAS LEHMAN/SHUTTERSTOCK ©

Below: Gettysburg Battlefield; Below left: Marker for a farm destroyed at Gettysburg; Below right: Statue of Union soldiers

National Mall & Memorial Parks

A nation is many things: its people, its history, its politics and its amassed knowledge. Somehow, each one of these is given architectural life on the National Mall, the center of iconography of the most iconic city in America. National Mall and Memorial Parks protects 14 sites on the mall, as well as other memorials in downtown Washington, DC.

Lincoln Memorial

Anchoring the Mall's west end is the hallowed **shrine to Abraham Lincoln** (📞20 2-426-6841; www.nps.gov/linc; 2 Lincoln Memorial Circle NW; ⊙24hr), who gazes across the Reflecting Pool beneath his neoclassical, Doric-columned abode. The words of his Gettysburg Address and Second Inaugural speech flank the huge marble statue on the north and south walls. On the steps, Martin Luther King Jr delivered his famed 'I Have a Dream' speech; look for the engraving that marks the spot (it's on the landing 18 stairs from the top).

Washington Monument

Peaking at 555ft (and 5in) and composed of 36,000 blocks of stone, the **Washington Monument** (www.nps.gov/wamo; 2 15th St NW; 🚌Circulator National Mall) is the district's tallest structure. Political shenanigans followed by the Civil War interrupted its construction. When work began anew, a

new quarry sourced the marble; note the delineation in color where the old and new marble meet about a third of the way up. Repairs on the monument, completed in 2019, involved an update of the elevator system and the opening of a new security screening facility.

Vietnam Veterans Memorial

Maya Lin's design for this hugely evocative memorial takes the form of a black, low-lying 'V' – an expression of the psychic scar wrought by the Vietnam War. The **monument** (www.nps.gov/vive; 5 Henry Bacon Dr NW; ⊙24hr) descends into the earth, with the names of the war's 58,000-plus American casualties – listed in the order they died – chiseled into the dark, reflective wall. It's a subtle but profound monument – and all the more surprising as Lin was only 21 when she designed it.

Ford's Theatre National Historic Site

On April 14, 1865, John Wilkes Booth assassinated Abraham Lincoln at **Ford's Theatre** (📞202-347-4833; www.fords.org; 511 10th St NW, Penn Quarter; ⊙9am-4:30pm). Free timed-entry tickets provide access to the site, which has four parts: the theater itself (where you see the box seat Lincoln was sitting in when Booth shot him), the basement museum (displaying Booth's .44-caliber pistol, his muddy boot etc), Petersen House (across the street, where Lincoln died) and the aftermath exhibits. Arrive early (by 8:30am) because tickets do run out. Better yet, reserve online to ensure admittance.

Belmont-Paul Women's Equality National Monument

This brick **house** (📞202-546-1210; www.nps. gov/bepa; 144 Constitution Ave NE, Capitol Hill; ⊙9am-5pm Wed-Sun), only steps from the US Capitol, may not look like much, but throughout the 20th century it was ground zero for women fighting for their rights.

Below: Ford's Theatre

JOHN M. CHASE/SHUTTERSTOCK ©

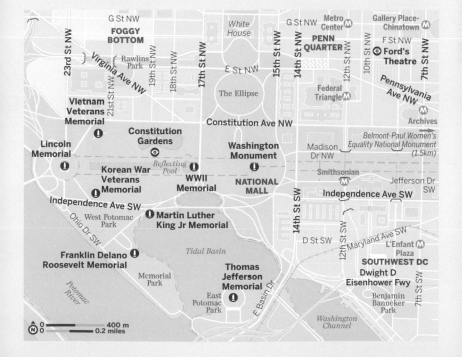

Multimillionaire socialite and suffragist Alva Belmont purchased the house in 1929 for the National Woman's Party headquarters. Activist Alice Paul lived here for 43 years, spearheading rallies and demonstrations. Designated a national monument in 2016, it's now a house museum filled with fascinating artifacts celebrating the women's fight for equality.

Martin Luther King Jr Memorial

Opened in 2011, this was the first Mall **memorial** (www.nps.gov/mlkm; 1964 Independence Ave SW; ⊘24hr) to honor an African American. Sculptor Lei Yixin carved the piece, which is reminiscent in concept and style of the Mt Rushmore memorial. Besides Dr King's striking, 30ft-tall image, known as

the **Stone of Hope**, there are two blocks of granite behind him that represent the Mountain of Despair. A wall inscribed with King's powerful quotes about democracy, justice and peace flanks the piece.

Constitution Gardens

Constitution Gardens (www.nps.gov/coga; Constitution Ave NW; ⊘24hr) is a bit of a locals' secret. Quiet, shady and serene, it's a reminder of the size of the Mall – how can such isolation exist amid so many tourists? Here's the simple layout: a copse of trees set off by a small kidney-shaped pool, punctuated by a tiny island holding the **Signers' Memorial**, a stone platform honoring those who signed the Declaration of Independence.

elow: Vietnam Veterans Memorial, designed by Maya Lin; Below left: Lincoln Memorial; Below right: Washington Monument

GIUSEPPECRIMENI, SHUTTERSTOCK ©

ROB CRANDALL/SHUTTERSTOCK ©

Franklin Delano Roosevelt Memorial

The 7.5-acre **memorial** (www.nps.gov/frde; 400 W Basin Dr SW; ⊘24hr) pays tribute to the longest-serving president in US history. Visitors are taken through four red-granite areas that narrate FDR's time in office, from the Depression to the New Deal to WWII. The story is told through statuary and inscriptions, punctuated with fountains and peaceful alcoves. It's especially pretty at night, when the marble shimmers in the glossy stillness of the Tidal Basin.

Thomas Jefferson Memorial

Set on the south bank of the Tidal Basin amid the cherry trees, this **memorial** (⏰20 2-426-6841; www.nps.gov/thje; 13 E Basin Dr SW; ⊘24hr) honors the third US president, political philosopher, drafter of the Declaration of Independence and founder of the University of Virginia. Designed by John Russell Pope in the style of the ancient Roman Pantheon, the rounded, open-air monument was initially derided by critics as 'the Jefferson Muffin.' Inside is a 19ft bronze likeness, and excerpts from Jefferson's writings are etched into the walls.

World War II Memorial

Dedicated in 2004, this grandiose memorial honors the 16 million US soldiers who served in **WWII** (www.nps.gov/wwii; 17th St SW; ⊘24hr). Groups of veterans regularly come here to pay their respects to the 400,000 Americans who died as a result of the conflict. The plaza's dual arches symbolize victory in the Atlantic and Pacific theaters, and the 56 surrounding pillars represent each US state and territory.

Korean War Veterans Memorial

Nineteen steel soldiers wander through clumps of juniper past a wall bearing images of the 'Forgotten War' that assemble, in the distance, into a panorama of the Korean mountains. The **memorial** (www.nps.gov/kwvm; 10 Daniel French Dr SW; ⊘24hr) is best visited at night, when the sculpted patrol – representing all races and combat branches that served in the war – takes on a phantom cast. In winter, when snow folds over the infantry's field coats, the impact is especially powerful.

African American Civil War Memorial

Standing at the center of a granite plaza, this bronze memorial (www.afroamcivilwar.org; cnr U St NW & Vermont Ave NW, U Street; ⊘24hr), Spirit of Freedom, depicting rifle-bearing troops is DC's first major art piece by black sculptor Ed Hamilton. The statue is surrounded on three sides by the **Wall of Honor**, listing the names of 209,145 African American troops who fought in the Union army, as well as the 7000 white soldiers who served alongside them.

George Mason Memorial

This little oasis of flowers and fountains honors the famed **statesman** (www.nps.gov/gemm; cnr Ohio Dr & E Basin Dr SW; ⊘24hr; ☐Circulator, ⓂOrange, Silver, Blue Line to Smithsonian) and author of the Commonwealth of Virginia Declaration of Rights (a forerunner to the US Bill of Rights). Wendy M Ross' bronze sculpture of Mason sits (literally; his legs are crossed and the man looks eminently relaxed) on a marble bench under a pretty covered arcade. His wise words against slavery and in support of human rights are incised in the bench.

Below: World War II Memorial; Bottom: George Mason Memorial

ESB PROFESSIONAL/SHUTTERSTOCK ©

New River Gorge National Park

The New River is actually one of the oldest in the world, and the primeval forest gorge it runs through is one of the most breathtaking in the Appalachians. The National Park Service protects a stretch of the New River that falls 750ft over 50 miles.

Great For...

State
West Virginia

Entrance Fee
Free

Area
109 sq miles (53 miles long)

A compact set of rapids up to Class V is concentrated at the northernmost end of the park. The region is an adventure mecca, with world-class white-water runs and challenging single-track trails. Rim and gorge hiking trails offer beautiful views.

White-water Rafting

White-water rafting is fantastic on the New River, with rapids appropriate for families as well as thrill-seekers. Rafting the nearby Gauley River during its fall dam release is one of the most exciting white-water adventures in the US.

With great scenery and low-key rapids, the **New River** works well for newbie paddlers and families. Kids can hop into duckies to explore the mild waves of the Upper New while the whole family can have fun running the 20 or so easy rapids on the Lower New.

Your eight-person raft looks pretty darn flimsy in the moments just before you

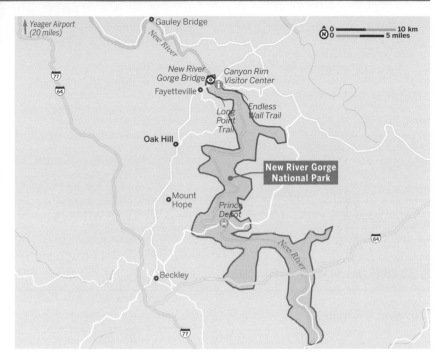

launch into the raging **Gauley River** during the annual fall dam release – when the Army Corps of Engineers expels flood-level waters into the river. These releases take place on weekends in September and October, a period of time known in these parts as Gauley Season. One of the most thrilling rafting adventures in the world, a fall ride on the Gauley begins at the base of the Summersville Dam then crashes through 100 rapids as the river plunges 668ft over 25 miles. Guided trips usually take a half-day and cover half of the 25-mile run, with paddlers tackling either the Upper Gauley or the Lower.

Thrills on the wild Upper Gauley include numerous Class III to V+ rapids plus a final drop down a 12ft drop! You must be at least 16 years old for this trip. Only slightly less thrilling is the 12-mile Lower Gauley, which challenges paddlers with 70 rapids ranging from Class III to V. Trips on the Gauley are still fun and challenging in summer, just not

as gobsmackingly thrilling as trips during Gauley Season.

The eastern edge of the Gauley River National Recreation Area (www.nps.gov/gari) is about 20 miles north of the New River via US 19. The larger rafting outfitters offer campsites and cabins for overnight stays and some have a restaurant or two, all clustered within woodsy adventure complexes near one of the rivers.

Climbing

Hard sandstone cliffs line the gorge, reaching heights of 120ft and drawing rock climbers with their 1400 established climbs. Climbing season runs April through November. Most routes are 5.9 and harder, and are best tackled by advanced climbers. For gear and guides, start in Fayetteville.

Hiking

Trails unfurl through thick forests running above and alongside the river. Panoramic views and tree-framed glimpses of the New

River Gorge Bridge are highlights. You'll also find trails in the state parks along the river. For a quick look at the gorge bridge, head to the **Canyon View Boardwalk** behind the Canyon Rim Visitor Center (p97). This short trail has upper and lower viewpoints, the latter reached by a steep descent on stairs. You'll pass great views of the gorge on the 5-mile round-trip **Endless Wall Trail** (www.nps.gov/neri/planyourvisit/hiking. htm), which begins off Lansing-Edmond Rd about 1.3 miles south of US 19. It also leads to top-notch rock-climbing sites. Several good trails begin east of Fayetteville off Gatewood Rd. The 1.6-mile **Long Point Trail** (www.nps.gov/neri/planyourvisit/fayette ville_trails.htm; Newtown Rd, off Gatewood Rd)

ends with a great view of the gorge bridge from a rocky outcrop.

Mountain Biking

The Boy Scouts built the four mountain-bike loops comprising the **Arrowhead Trails**, which are located in the New River Gorge about 3.5 miles east of Fayetteville. These four loops range from easy to intermediate and cover almost 13 miles. Check out the New River Gorge website (www.nps.gov/neri) for more details and a full list of all the biking trails in the park, including updates about closures and trail conditions. Biking in the gorge is permitted on designated trails only. Most of the Long Point Trail is open to mountain biking.

Essential Information

Sleeping & Eating

There is no lodging in the park. The only camping available is free primitive camping near the river, with no drinking water or hookups. Many outdoor outfitters offer a mix of campsites and cabins near the river that are a convenient choice before an early-morning rafting trip. For more traditional lodging options head to Fayetteville or the lodge at **Hawks Nest State Park** (✆304-658-5212; www.hawksnestsp.com; 49 Hawks Nest Park Rd).

There are no park-run restaurants but you will find restaurants and bars on the grounds of the larger outdoor outfitters. These are typically open to the general public. Drive to Fayetteville for a mix of good eateries.

Visitor Center

For information about history, geology and recreation, stop by the Canyon Rim

Visitor Center (p97), one of four NPS visitor centers along the New River. A short trail behind the building leads to a leaf-framed view of the graceful New River Gorge Bridge, which sits 876ft above the river and is the third-highest bridge in the US. It carries traffic on US 19.

Getting There & Away

The **Yeager Airport** (✆304-344-8033; https://yeagerairport.com; 100 Airport Rd) in Charleston is located 70 miles northwest.

Amtrak (www.amtrak.com) stops at three places in the NPS region on the Cardinal route, which runs between Chicago, Washington, DC, and New York City. One of these stops is the **Prince Depot** (✆800-872-7245; www.amtrak.com; 5034 Stanaford Rd, Prince), which is 23 miles south of Fayetteville near Beckley. Greyhound (www. greyhound.com) stops in Beckley at 360 Prince St.

Top left: Summersville Dam; Top right: New River Gorge Bridge; Bottom: Endless Wall Trail

MALACHI JACOBS/SHUTTERSTOCK ©

FRANCISCO BLANCO/SHUTTERSTOCK ©

SEAN PAVONE/SHUTTERSTOCK ©

Across the Appalachian Trail

The Appalachian Trail runs 2175 miles from Maine to Georgia, across the original American frontier and some of the oldest mountains on the continent. Initially built by private citizens, it is today managed as a National Scenic Trail in collaboration between the National Park Service, US Forest Service, Appalachian Trail Conservancy, numerous state agencies and thousands of volunteers. This journey fleshes out the unique ecological-cultural sphere of the greater Appalachians, particularly in Maryland, West Virginia and Virginia. Get your hiking boots on and get ready for sun-dappled national forests, quaint tree-shaded towns and many a wild, unfettered mountain range.

Distance 495 miles

Duration 5 days

Best Time to Go
September to November; brisk fall air is good for hikes.

Essential Photo
The New River Gorge Bridge from the visitor center trail.

Best for Culture
Live music at the Purple Fiddle.

❶ Harpers Ferry
Harpers Ferry, a postcard-perfect little town nestled between the Shenandoah and Potomac Rivers, is home to some of the most beautiful scenery along the Appalachian Trail. Conveniently, this is also the headquarters for the Appalachian Trail Conservancy. The visitor center is located in the heart of town on Washington St and is a great place to ask for advice about how best to explore this region.

For all that West Virginia is associated with the Appalachian Trail, it's only home to a scant 4 miles of it. However, the scenery is so awe-inspiring that it would be a shame to miss it. Take a hike framed by the wild rushing rapids of the Potomac River below, and the craggy, tree-covered mountain peaks above. If you're hiking from Maryland, you'll cross the Potomac River on a footbridge and then the Shenandoah River to pass into Virginia. While in West Virginia proper, stop at the famed **Jefferson Rock**, an ideal place for a picnic.

The Drive » Head west from Harpers Ferry on US 340 for about 3 miles, then turn right onto WV 230N. It's about 9 miles from here to Shepherdstown. Parking downtown is heavily regulated because of the nearby college, so either park a few blocks away and hoof it, or bring coins for the meters.

❷ Shepherdstown
Shepherdstown is one of many settlements in the mountains cut from a similar cloth – artsy college towns that balance a significant amount of natural beauty with a quirky, bohemian culture. This is the oldest town in West Virginia, founded in 1762, and its **historic district** is packed with Federal-style brick buildings that are heartrendingly cute.

The bulk of the best-preserved buildings can be found along German St; all of the cutest historical twee-ness is within walking distance of here. The historic center is also close to Shepherd University; the student presence can be felt pretty strongly in town, but it's balanced out by plenty of pick-up-driving West Virginia locals.

The city is a convenient base for exploring the region, and there are lots of great restaurants here.

The Drive » Head west on WV 45 (the Martinsburg Pike) for around 8 miles. Then

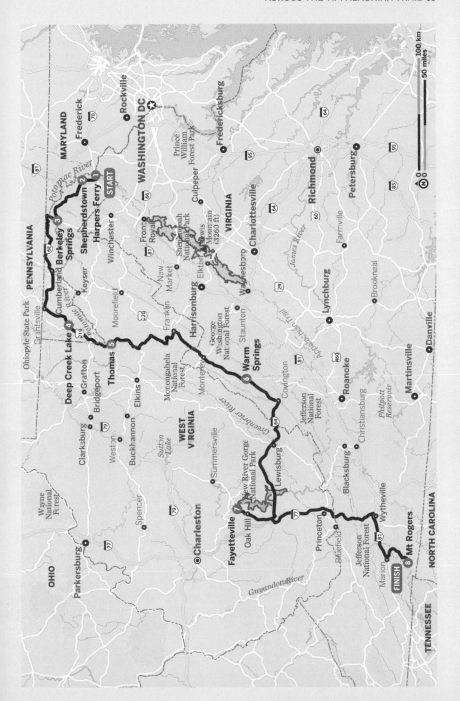

turn right onto US 11 N/WV 9W (which quickly becomes just WV 9) and follow it to the northwest, through the mountains, for 24 miles. Follow signs for Berkeley Springs.

❸ Berkeley Springs

Welcome to one of America's original spa towns, a mountainside retreat that's been a holiday destination since Colonial times. (Did George Washington sleep here? You bet.) The draw has always been the warm mineral springs, long rumored to have healing properties; such rumors have attracted a mix of people, from country folk with pickup trucks and gun racks to hippie refugees from the '60s.

Although it's still best known for its spas, one of the more enjoyable activities here is strolling around and soaking up the odd New-Age-crystal-therapy-meets-mountain-folk vibe. If you do need a pamper, head out to **Berkeley Springs State Park**

(☎304-258-2711; www.berkeleyspringssp.com; 2 S Washington St; 30min bath $27, 1hr massage $99-129; ⊙9am-6pm) and relax in its Roman Bath House and spring-fed pools.

Keep an eye out for the Samuel Taylor Suit Cottage, more popularly known as **Berkeley Castle**. Perched on a hill above town, it looks like a European fortress and was built in 1885 for Colonel Samuel Taylor Suit of Washington, DC.

The Drive » Head into Maryland by going north on US 522 for about 6 miles; take the exit toward US 40/I-68 westbound. Follow this road west for around 62 miles through Maryland's western mountain spine. Take MD 495 south for 3½ miles, then turn right onto Glendale Rd and follow it to Deep Creek Lake.

❹ Deep Creek Lake

Deep in Western Maryland, plunked into a blue valley at the end of a series

Below: Jefferson Rock; Below left: Berkeley Springs; Below right: Shepherdstown

of tree-ridged mountains, is Maryland's largest lake: Deep Creek. With some 69 miles of shoreline stretching through the hills, there's a lot of outdoor activities here, as well as a small town for lodging and food. Try to arrive in October, when the **Autumn Glory Festival** (www.visitdeepcreek. com; ☻mid-Oct) celebrates the shocking fire hues of crimson and orange that paint a swath across the local foliage. The **Garrett County Visitor Center** (✆301-387-4386; www.visitdeepcreek.com; 15 Visitors Center Dr, McHenry; ☻9am-5pm) is a good launching point for exploring the region.

The lake is most easily accessed via **Deep Creek Lake State Park** (✆301-387-5563; http://dnr.maryland.gov/publiclands; 898 State Park Rd, Swanton; per vehicle $5 Jun-Aug, per person $5 Sep-May; ☻8am-sunset; P♿☺), which sits on a large plateau known as the Tablelands. The area is carpeted in oak and hickory forest, and black bear sightings, while uncommon, are not unheard of. Nearby is **Swallow Falls State Park** (✆301-387-6938; http://dnr.maryland.gov/publiclands; 2470 Maple Glade Rd; per person $5 Jun-Aug and Sat & Sun May, Sep & Oct, per vehicle $5 rest of year; ☻8am-sunset Mar-Oct, from 10am Nov-Feb; P♿☺), one of the most rugged, spectacular parks in the state. Hickory and hemlock trees hug the Youghiogheny River, which cuts a white line through wet slate gorges. On site is the 53ft Muddy Creek Falls, the highest free-falling waterfalls in the state.

The Drive » Take US 219 southbound out of Garrett County and into West Virginia. You'll be climbing though some dramatic mountain scenery on the way. Once you cross the George Washington Hwy, you're almost in West Virginia. It's about 30 miles from Deep Creek Lake to Thomas.

⑤ Thomas

The side-by-side towns of Thomas and Davis aren't more than a blip on the... where'd they go? Oh, there they are. The big business of note for travelers here is the **Purple Fiddle** (✆304-463-4040; www.purplefiddle.com; 96 East Ave, Thomas; tickets $7-20; ☻11am-8pm Sun-Thu, to midnight Fri & Sat), a great mountain store where bluegrass culture and artsy day-trippers from the urban South and Northeast mash up into a stomping good time. There's live music every night; you may want to purchase tickets for weekend shows in advance. The Fiddle is an unexpected surprise out here, and a fun one at that. There are a couple of good microbreweries and small lodgings across the two towns. Davis is 12 miles north of **Canaan Valley Resort** (✆304-866-4121; www.canaanresort.com; 230 Main Lodge Rd; lift tickets adult/youth 6-12yr/child $68/44/free; ♿).

About 5 miles south of Thomas is **Blackwater Falls State Park** (✆304-259-5216; www.blackwaterfalls.com; 1584 Blackwater Lodge Rd; P) FREE. The falls tumble into an 8-mile gorge lined by red spruce, hickory and hemlock trees. There are loads of hiking options; look for the **Pendleton Point Overlook**, which perches over the deepest, widest point of the Canaan Valley.

The Drive » From Thomas, take the Appalachian Hwy south. The numerical and name designation of the road will switch a few times, from US 33 to WV 28 and back. After about 50 miles, turn right onto US 220 and follow for 31 miles to Warm Springs. This drive is beautiful; take your time and enjoy.

⑥ Warm Springs

There's barely a gas station in sight out here, let alone a mall. You've crossed back into Virginia, and are now in the middle of the 1.8-million-acre **George Washington & Jefferson National Forests** (✆540-839-2521; www.fs.usda.gov/gwj; 422 Forestry Rd, Hot Springs; tent & RV sites with/without electricity $17/12, day use area fee per vehicle $3, primitive camping free; ☻8am-4:30pm Mon-Fri). We have provided details for the Warm Springs Ranger District, one of eight districts managing this enormous protected area, which stretches from Virginia to Kentucky.

There are far too many trails in this area to list here. Note that most trails in the region are not actually in the town of Warm Springs; there is a ranger office here, and staff can direct you to the best places to explore. Some favorites include the 1-mile **Brushy Ridge Trail**, which wends past abundant blueberry and huckleberry bushes, and the 2.3-mile **Gilliam Run Trail**, which ascends to the top of Beard Mountain.

The Drive » Take US 220 southbound over more mountain peaks, by more hamlets all the way to I-64. Then take the highway west for around 40 miles. Exit onto US 60 westbound and drive for 35 miles, then merge onto US 19. Follow it for 7 miles over the New River Gorge to Fayetteville.

❼ Fayetteville

You've crossed state lines yet again, and are back in West Virginia. Little Fayetteville serves as the gateway to the **New River Gorge**, a canyon cut by a river that is ironically one of the oldest rivers in North America. Some 70,000 acres of the gorge are gazetted as national parkland. **Canyon Rim Visitor Center** (📞304-574-2115; www.nps.gov/neri; 162 Visitor Center Rd, Lansing; ⏰9am-5pm; 🎫) ♿, just north of the impressive **gorge bridge** (www.nps.gov/neri; Hwy 19; 🅿) **FREE**, is one of four National Park Service visitor centers along the river and offers information about river outfitters, gorge climbing, hiking and mountain biking, as well as white-water rafting to the north on the Gauley River. A short trail behind the visitor center leads to great views of the photogenic bridge, the third-highest bridge in the US.

If you're interested in rafting, consider contacting the professionals at **Cantrell Ultimate Rafting** (📞304-877-8235; www.cantrellultimaterafting.com; 49 Cantrell Dr; rafting from $89).

The Drive » Take US 19 south for 15 miles until you can merge with I-64/77 (it eventually becomes just I-77) southbound. Take this road south for 75 miles, then get on I-81 south and follow it for 27 miles to Marion.

❽ Mt Rogers

You'll end this trip at the highest mountain in Virginia (and yes, you've crossed state lines again!). There are plenty of trekking opportunities in the **Mt Rogers National Recreation Area** (www.fs.usda.gov/gwj; Hwy 16, Marion), part of the Washington & Jefferson National Forests. Contact the **ranger office** (📞276-783-5196, 800-628-7202; www.fs.usda.gov; 3714 Hwy 16, Marion; ⏰8am-4:30pm Mon-Fri) for information on summiting the peak of Mt Rogers (5729ft), and pat yourself on the back for getting here after so many state border hops! The local **Elk Garden Trailhead** is one of the best access points for tackling the local wilderness, and intersects the actual Appalachian Trail, making for an appropriate finish to the trip.

KHANIM/SHUTTERSTOCK ©

Swallow Falls

CLASSIC ROAD TRIPS

Blue Ridge Parkway

Running through Virginia and North Carolina, the Blue Ridge National Scenic Byway is the most visited area of national parkland in the USA, attracting almost 20 million road-trippers a year. 'America's Favorite Drive' meanders through quintessentially bucolic pasturelands and imposing Appalachian vistas, past college towns and mountain hamlets. This trip threads into and off the parkway, exploring all of the above and some back roads in between.

Distance 185 miles

Duration 3 days

Best Time to Go
June through October for great weather and open amenities.

Essential Photo
A panorama of the Blue Ridge Mountains from Sharp Top, Peaks of Otter.

Best for Culture
Staunton is a food and arts hub.

❶ Staunton
Our trip starts in a place we'd like to end. End up retiring, that is. There are some towns in the USA that just, for lack of a better term, *nail it*, and Staunton is one of them. Luckily, it serves as a good base for exploring the upper parkway.

So what's here? A pedestrian-friendly and handsome center; more than 200 of the town's buildings were designed by noted Victorian architect TJ Collins, hence Staunton's attractive uniformity. There's an artsy yet unpretentious bohemian vibe thanks to the presence of two things: Mary Baldwin, a small women's liberal arts college, and the gem of the Shenandoah mountains: **Blackfriars Playhouse** (☎540-851-1733; www.americanshakespearecenter. com; 10 S Market St; tickets $29-49). This is the world's only re-creation of Shakespeare's original indoor theater. The facility hosts the immensely talented American Shakespeare Center company, with performances throughout the year. See a show here. It will do you good.

History buffs should check out the **Woodrow Wilson Presidential Library** (☎540-885-0897; www.woodrowwilson.org; 18 N Coalter St; adult/student/child 6-12yr $14/7/5; ⊙9am-5pm Mon-Sat, from noon Sun Mar-Oct, to 4pm Nov-Feb) across town. Stop by and tour the hilltop Greek Revival house where Wilson grew up, which has been faithfully restored to its original 1856 appearance.

By this point you'll probably be dreaming of ditching your 9-to-5 job and moving to the country. A good way to snap yourself out of this fantasy is by visiting the **Frontier Culture Museum** (☎540-332-7850; www. frontiermuseum.org; 1290 Richmond Rd; adult/student/child 6-12yr $12/11/7; ⊙9am-5pm mid-Mar–Nov, 10am-4pm Dec–mid-Mar). The hard work of farming comes to life via the familiar Virginia trope of employing historically costumed interpreters. The museum has Irish, German and English farms to explore.

The Drive » From Staunton, take I-64E towards Richmond for about 15 miles. Take exit 99 to merge onto US 250/Three Notched Mountain Hwy heading east toward Afton, then follow the signs onto the Blue Ridge Parkway. Humpback Rocks is at Mile 5.8.

❷ Humpback Rocks
Had enough great culture and small-town hospitality? No? Tough, because we're

moving on to the main event: the Blue Ridge Pkwy. Now, we need to be honest with you: this is a weird trip. We're asking you to drive along the parkway, which slowly snakes across the peaks of the Appalachians, but every now and then we're going to ask you to detour off this scenic mountain road to, well, other scenic roads.

Anyways, we start at **Humpback Rocks** (www.nps.gov/blri; Mile 5.8, Blue Ridge Pkwy), the entrance to the Virginia portion of the parkway (252 miles of the 469-mile parkway are in North Carolina). You can tour 19th-century farm buildings or take the steep trail to the namesake Humpback Rocks, which offer spectacular 360-degree views across the mountains. The on-site visitor center is a good primer for the rest of your parkway experience.

The Drive » The next stretch of the trip is 39 miles on the parkway. Follow signs for US 60, then follow that road west for 10 miles to Lexington.

❸ Lexington

What? Another attractive university town set amid the forested mountains of the lower Shenandoah Valley? Well, why not.

In fact, while Staunton moderately revolves around Mary Baldwin, Lexington positively centers, geographically and culturally, around two schools: the **Virginia Military Institute** (VMI; www.vmi.edu; Letcher Ave) and **Washington & Lee University** (☑540-458-8400; www.wlu.edu; 204 West Washington St). VMI is the oldest state-supported military academy in the country, dedicated to producing the Classical ideal of citizen-soldiers; the ideals of this institution and the history of its cadet-students are explored at the **VMI Museum** (☑540-464-7334; www.vmi.edu/museum; 415 Letcher Ave; $5; ☺9am-5pm). While graduates do not have to become enlisted officers within the US military, the vast majority do so. In addition, the school's **George C Marshall Museum** (☑540-463-2083; www.marshall foundation.org/museum; VMI Pde; adult/student/

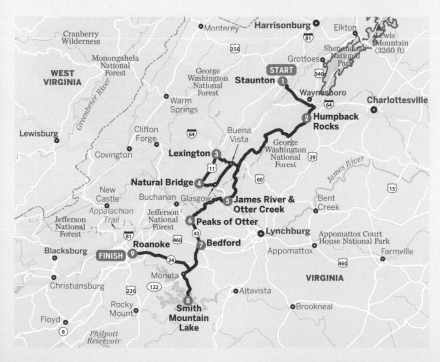

child under 13yr $5/2/free; ⊘11am-4pm Tue-Sat) honors the creator of the Marshall Plan for post-WWII European reconstruction.

VMI cadets can often be seen jogging around Lexington, perhaps casting a glance at the students at Washington & Lee, a decidedly less structured but no less academically respected school. The W&L campus includes the **Lee Chapel & Museum** (☑540-458-8768; www.wlu.edu/lee-chapel-and-museum; Washington & Lee University; donation adult/child $4/2; ⊘9am-4pm Mon-Sat, 1-4pm Sun Nov-Mar, to 5pm Apr-Oct), where the school's namesake, patron and Confederate general Robert E Lee, is buried. Lee's beloved horse, Traveller, is buried outside, and visitors often leave pennies as a sign of respect.

Just a few miles north on Rte 11 is **Hull's Drive-in movie theater** (☑540-463-2621; www.hullsdrivein.com; 2367 N Lee Hwy/US 11; adult/child 5-11yr $7/3; ⊘gates open 6:30pm Fri & Sat Mar-Oct; ⌖). This totally hardcore artifact of the golden age of automobiles is a living museum to the road trips your parents remember.

The Drive » Take US 11 southbound for about 12 miles to get to Natural Bridge (you can take I-81 as well, but it's not nearly as scenic and takes just as long).

❹ Natural Bridge

Before we send you back to the Blue Ridge Pkwy, stop by the gorgeous **Natural Bridge** (☑540-291-1326; www.dcr.virginia.gov; 6477 S Lee Hwy; adult/child 6-12yr $8/6; ⊘8am-9pm) and its wonderful potpourri of amusements. Natural Bridge is a legitimate natural wonder – and is even claimed to be one of the Seven Natural Wonders of the World, though just who put that list together remains unclear. Soaring 200ft in the air, this centuries-old rock formation lives up to the hype. Those who aren't afraid of a little religion should hang around for the 'Drama of Creation' light show that plays nightly underneath and around the bridge. Natural Bridge, formerly privately owned, became a state park in 2016.

The Drive » Head back to the Blue Ridge Parkway using US 60 and get on at Buena Vista. Drive about 13 miles south to the James River area near Mile 63.

❺ James River & Otter Creek

The next portion of the Blue Ridge Pkwy overlooks the road leading to Lynchburg. Part of the reason for that town's proximity is the James River, which marks the parkway's lowest elevation (650ft above sea level); the river was the original transportation route through the mountains.

This area is rife with hiking and sightseeing opportunities. **Otter Creek Trail** begins at a local campsite and runs for a moderately strenuous 3½ miles; you can access it at different points from overlooks at Mile 61.4, Mile 62.5 and Mile 63.1.

For a really easy jaunt, head to the **James River Visitor Center** at Mile 63.6 and take the 0.2-mile **James River Trail** to the restored James River and Kanawha Canal lock, built between 1845 and 1851. The visitor center has information on the history of the canal and its importance to local transportation. From here follow the **Trail of Trees**, which goes half a mile to a wonderful overlook on the James River.

The Drive » It's about 20 miles from here to Peaks of Otter along the Blue Ridge Pkwy. At Mile 74.7, the very easy 0.1-mile Thunder Ridge Trail leads to a pretty valley view. The tough 1.2-mile Apple Orchard Falls Trail can be accessed at Mile 78.4.

❻ Peaks of Otter

The three **Peaks of Otter** – Sharp Top, Flat Top and Harkening Hill – were once dubbed the highest mountains in North America by Thomas Jefferson. He was decidedly wrong in that assessment, but the peaks are undeniably dramatic, dominating the landscape for miles around.

There's a visitor center at Mile 86; from here you can take the steep 1½-mile **Sharp Top Trail** (one way) which summits the eponymous mountain (3875ft). The **Flat Top Trail** goes higher and further (5.4 miles round trip), but at a considerably less

Below: Blue Ridge Parkway; Below left: Natural Bridge; Below right: Lee Chapel

demanding incline. You'll end at the Peaks Picnic area (say that three times fast). If you're pressed for time, the 0.8-mile **Elk Run Trail** is an easy self-guided loop and nature tour.

At Mile 83.1, just before the visitor center, the **Fallingwater Cascades Trail** is a 1½-mile loop that wanders past deep-carved ravines to a snowy-white waterfall.

The Peaks of Otter Lodge sits prettily beside a lake at the base of the peaks.

The Drive ›› Get on VA 43 south, also known as Peaks Rd, from the Blue Ridge Pkwy. It's about an 11-mile drive along this road to Bedford.

❼ Bedford

Tiny Bedford suffered the most casualties per capita during WWII, and hence was chosen to host the **National D-Day Memorial** (☏540-586-3329; www.dday.org; 3 Overlord Circle; adult/student 6yr-college $10/6; ☉10am-5pm, closed Mon Dec-Feb). Among its towering arch and flower garden is a cast of bronze figures re-enacting the storming of the beach, complete with bursts of water symbolizing the hail of bullets the soldiers faced.

The surrounding countryside is speckled with vineyards. **Peaks of Otter Winery** (☏540-586-3707; www.peaksofotterwinery.com; 1218 Elmos Rd; ☉noon-5pm Apr-Dec, Sat & Sun Jan-Mar) stands out from other viticulture tourism spots with its focus on producing fruit wines (the chili pepper wine is, by the way, 'better for basting than tasting' according to management).

White Rock vineyards (☏540-890-3359; www.whiterockwines.com; 2117 Bruno Dr, Goodview; ☉noon-5pm Thu-Mon Apr–mid-Dec), on the other hand, is a more traditional winery. A few acres of green grapevines (well, green in the right season anyway) seem to erupt around a pretty house; if you head in for a tasting, we're fans of the White Mojo pinot gris.

Learn more about the many vineyards here via the **Bedford Wine Trail** (www.thebedfordwinetrail.com).

The Drive ›› Take VA 122 (Burks Hill Rd) southbound for about 13.5 miles. In Moneta, take a left onto State Route 608 and drive for 6 miles, then turn right onto Smith Mountain Lake Pkwy. Go 2 miles and you're at the park.

❽ Smith Mountain Lake

This enormous, 32-sq-mile reservoir is one of the most popular recreation spots in Southwest Virginia and the largest lake contained entirely within the borders of the commonwealth. Vacation rentals and water activities abound, as does development, and there are portions of this picturesque dollop that have been overwhelmed with rental units. Most lake access is via private property only.

This isn't the case at **Smith Mountain Lake State Park** (☏540-297-6066; www.dcr. virginia.gov/state-parks/smith-mountain-lake; 1235 State Park Rd, Huddleston; per vehicle $7; ☉8:15am-dusk), located on the north shore of the lake. Don't get us wrong – there are lots of facilities here if you need them, including a boat ramp, picnic tables, fishing piers, an amphitheater, camping sites and cabin rentals. But in general, the area within the state park preserves the natural beauty of this area. Thirteen hiking trails wind through the surrounding forests.

The nearby **Hickory Hill Winery** (☏540-296-1393; www.smlwine.com; 1722 Hickory Cove Lane, Moneta; ☉noon-6pm Wed-Sun Apr-Oct, noon-5pm Sat Nov-Mar), anchored by a charming 1923 farmhouse, is a lovely spot to lounge about sipping on merlot either before or after your adventures on the lake.

The Drive ›› Head back toward Bedford on VA 122 and take a left on State Route 801/ Stony Fork Rd. Follow this to VA 24/Stewartsville Rd and take that road west about 20 miles to Roanoke.

❾ Roanoke

Roanoke is the largest city and commercial hub of Southwest Virginia. It's not as picturesque as other towns, but it's a good logistical base. The busy **Center in the Square** (📞540-342-5700; www. centerinthesquare.org; 1 Market Sq; ⏰10am-5pm Mon, to 8pm Tue-Sat, 1-6pm Sun) is the city's cultural heartbeat, with a science museum and planetarium, local history museum and theater. The striking **Taubman Museum of Art** (📞540-342-5760; www.taubmanmuseum. org; 110 Salem Ave SE; ⏰10am-5pm Wed-Sat, noon-5pm Sun, 10am-9pm 1st Fri of month; 🅿) **FREE**, a few blocks away, hosts excellent temporary exhibits.

The Drive » From Roanoke, you can hop back on the parkway and continue on into the Meadows of Dan portion of the park.

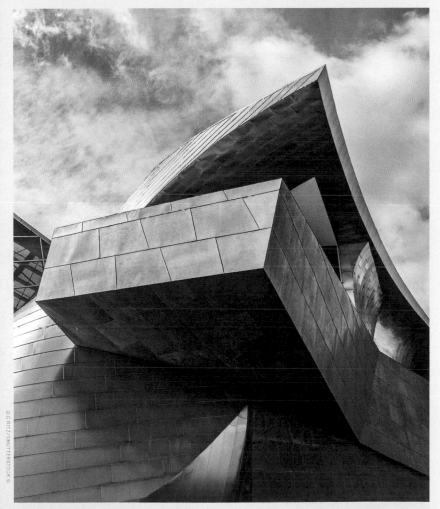

Taubman Museum of Art/Architect: Randall Stout

© C RITZ/SHUTTERSTOCK ©

In Focus

Below: Stone shelter, Old Rag Mountain; Right: White-tailed deer, Shenandoah National Park

STEVE HEAP/SHUTTERSTOCK ®

The Parks Today

New England and the Mid-Atlantic are home to some of the continent's best loved green spaces. But significant challenges are being faced due to high visitor numbers and climate change, with more powerful storms, higher temperatures and rising sea levels affecting every park. On a positive note, the parks received much-needed funding thanks to a landmark bill passed by Congress in 2020.

The Ravages of Climate Change

Climate change poses threats to every national park in the US. Devastating fires, floods and deadly temperatures have now become regular occurrences, and some parks face an existential crisis (Glacial National Park without glaciers, Joshua Tree without its eponymous trees). More powerful hurricanes have devastated parks in the east, including vast swaths of Gateway National Recreation Area, which saw record-breaking destruction during Hurricane Sandy in 2012.

In 2021 flash floods wiped out a trail in Acadia that had been used by indigenous Wabanaki hunters for centuries. Park officials described it as one of the most extreme weather events in its history. Rising sea levels have caused rapidly accelerating erosion on Cape Cod National Seashore, with beaches on the outer cape losing about 5 acres of shoreline each year. Ris-

DOTHOWK/GETTY IMAGES ©

ing temperatures have also impacted plant and animal life. Milder winters in Shenandoah among other parks has meant fewer days below freezing, which in turn has allowed invasive species to survive and spread.

Great American Outdoors Act

In 2020, during a rare moment of bipartisan agreement, the US Congress passed one of the most important land conservation acts in more than a generation. The Great American Outdoors Act allocated $9.5 billion over five years to national parks, forests, wildlife refuges and other federal lands. It also set aside $900 million to the Land & Water Conservation Fund, which can be used to purchase additional park land. Funding for the bill comes from revenues from oil and gas on non-public lands and waters – an aspect that critics describe as protecting national parks at the expense of the climate.

The money was desperately needed. Park attendance has increased by 50% since 1980, though the operation budget of the national park service has remained relatively flat. The backlog on much-needed repairs is staggering. Some $17 million was needed for maintenance on the Appalachian Trail. Cape Cod National Seashore had $55 million of repairs on the docket for roads, buildings and other structures, while Acadia required $25 million for improvements on wastewater systems, bridges and other essentials.

Loved to Death

Many of the national parks continue to draw record-breaking crowds. After a brief downturn during the early months of the COVID-19 pandemic, visitor numbers have rebounded to more than 300 million people per year. The Blue Ridge Parkway continues to be the most visited site in the national park system, drawing over 15 million people annually. Larger crowds have placed bigger strains on the parks, affecting everything from trash pickups to traffic congestion.

One proposed solution by the Sierra Club to help ease the bottlenecks is to create more national parks. Apart from lessening pressure on existing sites, this would draw attention to other outstanding destinations, and protect more lands under the park system. Earning national park status is a game changer. After the New River Gorge was named the US's 63rd national park in late 2020, a record number of visitors came the following year. Some locals worried the park was not equipped to handle the influx of visitors, with a lack of campgrounds, trails and parking spaces for the increasing crowds. Conservationists, however, celebrated its designation while also touting the job growth and economic benefits to local communities.

Monument Cove, Acadia National Park

History

The story begins in primordial times when clashing supersized continents created the Appalachian Mountains, among the oldest on the planet. Humans have also left their mark on these ancient landscapes. Nomadic tribes were the first to the area, followed by early settlers, loggers, coal miners and later nature lovers who helped safeguard these diverse landscapes for future generations.

20,000 BC
Sheets of glacial ice cover a northern swath of North America. Plant and animal species migrate to the southern Appalachia region.

9000 BC
Early nomadic peoples hunt game seasonally in the Appalachian Mountains and fish in waters off the East Coast.

1491
One year before Columbus crosses the Atlantic, the eastern seaboard is covered with farms, cleared lands and densely populated villages.

Early Peoples

In the beginning there was ice – at least as far as the land now known as New England, New York and northern parts of the USA was concerned. Roughly 20,000 years ago – just as humans were crossing the Bering land bridge from Asia into the Americas – the region was covered in glaciers, some 5000ft thick. The summit of mile-high Mt Katahdin in Maine would have risen just above the ice sheet, with all else a frozen and impenetrable panorama.

As the planet warmed, the ice retreated, and around 11,500 years ago fur-clad Stone Age hunters found their way into the valleys, across boulder-strewn hillsides and over vast wetlands. There were also grassy plains where woolly mammoths roamed and pockets of coniferous forest emerged from the tundra. This landscape would change dramatically over the next 9000 years. The changing scenery brought new food sources (including deer, otter, beaver and bear), and new technologies allowed for the grinding and milling of plants, as well as storage techniques for roots and nuts.

South of the Laurentide Ice Sheet, nomadic peoples lived in the Appalachia region since prehistoric times, leaving behind traces of their presence that are still being discovered by archaeologists. Among the finds are 13,000-year-old hunting projectiles found in the New River region. These were used to hunt now-extinct mastodon, bison and caribou species along likely animal migration paths. Ceramics from these early people date back to 700 BC, with primitive agricultural sites dating as far back as 1000 years ago.

European Arrival

When the first European settlers arrived in the New World, they encountered Native American inhabitants, mostly Algonquians, organized into small regional tribes. The northern tribes were solely hunter-gatherers, while the southern tribes hunted and practiced slash-and-burn agriculture, growing corn, squash and beans. The clash of cultures soon proved fatal to the Native American way of life. Two centuries later, the regional tribes were all but gone. European explorers left diseases in their wake to which indigenous peoples had no immunity. More destructive than any other factor – war, slavery or famine – disease epidemics devastated Native American populations by 90%.

Colonization & Settlement

The first settlers began arriving in the Appalachia region in the late 18th century, occupying lands that had once belonged to the Cherokee, Iroquois, Monacan, Saponi and Tutelo and many other tribes. Life on the Appalachian frontier was a constant struggle for survival in the wilderness. Settlers cut down trees to build log cabins and fences (as well as provide much-needed heat for the bitterly cold winters). They toiled to clear land for farming (not an easy task with boulders often buried in the soil) and built farmhouses, corncribs and smokehouses. The land had rich soil and proved ideal for growing important crops such as corn, wheat, rye, oats, flax and sorghum.

1607	**1614**	**1830**
Jamestown becomes the first permanent English settlement when colonists put down roots on marshland in present-day Virginia.	Captain John Smith sails the North Atlantic, travels from Maine to Cape Cod, maps the coastline and dubs the region 'New England.'	President Andrew Jackson signs into law the Indian Removal Act, which forces Native Americans off their ancestral lands.

NPS Logo

The National Park Service adopted its official logo in 1951. Shaped like an arrowhead, it features a bison and sequoia tree set against a snow-capped peak in the background. The design incorporates three unique themes of the national parks: archaeological and historical values (the arrowhead), plant and animal life (the sequoia and bison), and scenery and recreation (mountains and water).

In the summer, farmers would hike their sheep or cattle up to mountain pastures where the animals could freely graze. Hogs were left to forage in the thick forests of oak, hickory and chestnut trees surrounding the settlers' homes. Homesteaders had to be entirely self-sufficient, although hunting, fishing and trapping supplemented their income and provided goods for bartering, bringing in the likes of coffee, sugar and salt, which the settlers couldn't produce themselves.

Aside from the daily struggles of putting food on the table, there were also ever-present threats around them: panthers and bears prowled in the forests, and packs of wolves sometimes devastated the pioneers' small herds. The settlers were generally on good terms with Native American tribes due to trade in food. By the early 1800s, however, the Cherokee and other groups had largely disappeared from the area, having been forced to cede all of their lands through various treaties.

As more settlers arrived, the growing collection of farmsteads turned into tiny villages, with the addition of blacksmith shops, gristmills, churches and later schoolhouses, post offices and dry-goods stores. Communities were tightly knit. Villagers knew each other well, and made a social event out of corn husking, preparing molasses and gathering chestnuts in autumn. They also helped out in times of need. When one settler died, the men would build a coffin, dig a grave and assist with the burial, while the women helped prepare the body. Everyone helped the family of the deceased, assisting around the farm, preparing meals and taking care of the small children. The men were also recruited to help build roads in the area, some of which followed old trails first created by Native Americans.

Although Black history has remained largely hidden in the Appalachia region, scholars have recently found that slavery existed in every county in Appalachia. By 1860 some 18% of Appalachian households 'owned' people who were enslaved, compared to 29% of Southern families elsewhere.

Civil War

By the mid-19th century, slavery divided the nation into two camps: those in favor (largely from the south) and those who wanted to outlaw the practice. In 1859 one such abolitionist, John Brown, hoped to spark a major rebellion of people who were enslaved when he and a band of 21 men invaded a federal armory, a rifle factory and arsenal in Harpers Ferry. The raid was a fiasco, with 10 of Brown's men killed during the assault, and six captured and hanged afterward – including Brown (five escaped). The well-publicized raid, however,

1861–65

American Civil War erupts between North and South. President Lincoln is assassination five days after the war's end.

1900s

Large-scale logging operations begin, creating new roads and boom towns and scarring the landscape.

1912–21

During the West Virginia Mine Wars, clashes between miners and coal companies culminate at the Battle of Blair Mountain in 1921.

became a polarizing force, leading to strengthening resolve among both abolitionists and proslavery Southerners as both camps prepared for war.

In April 1861 American Confederates attacked Fort Sumter in South Carolina – the first salvo in what would become the country's bloodiest conflict. Washington, DC, was a prized target and the front lines of fighting often came quite near the capital. Indeed, when the war began, city residents (including President Lincoln) remained fearful of a siege from the Confederates, whose campfires were visible just across the Potomac in Virginia.

Major battles occurred in Virginia and Maryland, which are today preserved as important historic sites by the National Park Service. Wilderness areas also featured prominently in the conflict. During the Gettysburg campaign of 1863, Confederate general Robert E Lee moved across the Blue Ridge Mountains, using the forested slopes to screen troop movements as he advanced northward. A present-day portion of Skyline Drive in Shenandoah National Park was heavily used by the Confederacy throughout the war as a launchpad for attacks on Union army sites. Many Southern soldiers fighting for Lee and Stonewall Jackson grew up in the Shenandoah Valley and had deep connections to the mountains – some even had homes in the current boundaries of the national park.

A Scarred Landscape

In the decades following the Civil War, a new industry began to emerge: logging. At first it started out small, with selective timber cutting carried out by local landowners in various parts of the Appalachian Mountains. Trees such as ash, poplar and cherry were cut down and sold to lumber mills in nearby towns. By 1900, however, industrialists saw enormous financial opportunities in the large stands of old-growth forest in the mountains and began buying up properties and commencing large-scale operations.

Companies laid down railroad tracks to transport timber, built large mills and created lumber towns that grew into sizable villages. Hundreds of miles of logging roads were blazed through the mountains. Logging boom towns arrived overnight. By the 1930s, some areas of old-growth forests in the southern Appalachia (including much of West Virginia) were completely cut down. With no remaining timber, logging operations ground to a halt, the mills closed and nearby towns were abandoned.

Coal mining also left deep scars in the landscape. Mines, rail lines and work towns sprouted around the New River in West Virginia, with poorly paid miners chipping away millions of tons of coal each year. As with lumber, the resources were soon depleted, and by the 1950s the vast underground coal reserves were no more. This was good news for the forests and rivers, which saw a remarkable recovery within a few decades.

The Great Depression & the CCC

The early 1930s was a devastating period for many in the US. The stock market crash of 1929 heralded dark days ahead, with bank collapses, crop failures brought on by drought,

1913–40	1919	1933–42
Philanthropist John D Rockefeller Jr donates 11,000 acres and 57 miles of the carriage roads he designed for the creation of Acadia NP.	Bootlegging flourishes in the Appalachian Mountains after the passage of the 18th Amendment, which bans alcohol.	President Roosevelt establishes the Civilian Conservation Corps; CCC workers plant over 3 billion trees throughout the US.

Abandoned Places

You can still find vestiges of an industrial past hidden in the forest near New River Gorge. Rising from the New River near Glade Creek, empty piers once supported a metal bridge (recycled for use during WWII) that carried narrow-gauge lumber-bearing trains. Nearby, a few stone foundations, now covered in moss and thick vines, are all that remain of the logging town of Hamlet, which was home to mills, a boarding house, church, school and several hundred residents. The forest has reclaimed the settlement, which is now located near the primitive campsites of Glade Creek.

Further upriver, Thurmond was a coal-mining boom town in the early 1900s, with saloons, restaurants, stores, banks, a movie theater and the oversized homes of coal barons. Some 15 passenger trains stopped here each day, serving up to 75,000 visitors a year. Today Thurmond is a ghost town – though a remarkably well-preserved one – where you can look for ghosts while taking a self-guided walking tour. Take care when exploring as the railroad tracks are still used by trains – indeed Amtrak's *Cardinal* still stops here.

North of Thurmond, a winding barely two-lane road leads to Nuttallburg, a mining community that was active from the 1870s until the early 20th century. Now listed on the National Register of Historic Places, Nuttallburg is a surprisingly intact coal-mining complex, with old equipment, coke ovens, oversized conveyors and railroad tracks surrounded by densely forested slopes.

and mass migrations of people from the countryside into the city in a desperate search for work. By 1933 over one in four working-age Americans were unemployed.

Despite the economic hardship – or in part because of it – the 1930s was a promising decade for the wild spaces of New England and the Mid-Atlantic. New national parks were added to America's protected areas, including Shenandoah in 1935 and the Blue Ridge Parkway the following year, and Skyline Drive was completed after nine years of construction in 1939. Many historic battlefields were also added to the national park system in the 1930s.

As the Great Depression swept across the nation in the early 1930s, President Roosevelt came up with an innovative solution to put people back to work. He created the Civilian Conservation Corps (CCC), which would serve two purposes: it would create jobs and it would help in the nation's reforestation. CCC camps were set up across the country, including in numerous national park sites. Over the course of its existence, more than 3 million people – mostly young men – worked for the corps, which ran from 1933 to 1942. They labored at a variety of jobs: constructing access roads and bridges, planting trees, blazing trails and building water systems and other essential park infrastructure. Some groups were even charged with raising trout to replenish fish-depleted streams.

The arrival of WWII brought an end to the CCC, the country's greatest public relief program. The camps were closed down and many became abandoned ghost towns amid the quickly encroaching forest. The forest workers went off to war, and the national park budget was slashed.

1950

The NPS is quietly desegregated. Many prospective African American visitors never learn of the change, and avoid the parks altogether.

1961

John F Kennedy establishes Cape Cod National Seashore, the first national park created out of privately owned land.

1963

Martin Luther King Jr leads the Civil Rights march on the National Mall in Washington, DC.

Evolution of the National Parks

The parks have undergone changes – some subtle, others seismic – since their early days. Cramped visitor centers that were once little more than dark chambers full of dusty taxidermy animals and uninspiring natural history signage have been transformed into modern, sustainably designed buildings aimed at accommodating a wide range of visitors, including people with disabilities.

Parks are also aiming to increase diversity – both among staff and visitors. For many years, park ranger jobs were the exclusive domain of men. Things slowly began changing in 1964 after the passage of title VII of the Civil Rights Act, which made it unlawful to discriminate against someone on the basis of race, color, national origin, sex or religion. Over the next decade, more women joined the National Park Service, though the female uniform (with stewardess-like miniskirts and tunics, plus optional go-go boots) wasn't retired until 1978. These days, around 37% of park service employees are women, which some former employees describe (along with reports of sexism, sexual harassment and even assault) as indicative of how the NPS is failing women.

Minorities have long been underrepresented in the national parks. African Americans make up less than 7% of the park's permanent full-time workforce, despite making up over 13% of the US population. Similarly, less than 6% of the NPS workforce are Latinos, despite composing nearly 19% of the population. Visitors are also overwhelmingly white. This is perhaps not surprising given the history of racism and discrimination that people of color faced when attempting to visit national park sites. Shenandoah, for instance, enforced segregation until 1950 and herded African American visitors into a separate camping and picnic area on Lewis Mountain. Even once segregation ended at the park, Black visitors still had to get there, contending with segregated restaurants, hotels and restaurants along the way. Meanwhile at all 150 state parks that opened during the Great Depression in the South, African Americans were simply denied entry.

Rather than sweep history under the rug, the National Park Service admits it has work to do (among other things, you can see an exhibition on the history of segregation at Shenandoah's Byrd Visitor Center). Leaders like Robert Stanton, who was the first and only African American director of the NPS, have served as role models for future generations, and the park continues to strategize about new ways to attract people of color to national parks, which belong to all Americans.

Volunteering

Want to join the 300,000 people already volunteering in the national parks? Every year volunteers contribute over 6.5 million hours of service to make these places better. To learn more about opportunities, visit www.volunteer.gov.

1996
Robert Stanton becomes the first African American NPS director. Five years later Fran P Mainella becomes its first woman director.

2015
President Obama launches an initiative that gives a free annual national parks pass to all fourth graders and their families.

2020
New River Gorge in West Virginia becomes the US's 63rd national park. The new designation increases visitor numbers by 24%.

Bar Harbor

Outdoor Activities

Mountains, coasts and forests set the stage for a wide variety of adventures. You can scramble up rocky cliffs to magnificent views over the Appalachians or bounce your way down swollen rivers amid the roar of white water. There's cycling along smooth forest paths and kayaking across mirror-like lakes. During the low season, enjoy crowd-free hiking trails and snowshoeing through wintery landscapes.

Hiking

Whether you have an irrepressible urge to climb a mountain or just want to get some fresh air, hiking in a national park is the single best way to experience the sublime beauty of this area. Even if you're only here for a short visit, be sure to include at least one hike in your itinerary. Trails range from flat, easy and short paths to longer, more strenuous endeavors. Many are excellent for families and there are even wheelchair-accessible trails (including Limberlost Trail in Shenandoah and Ship Harbor Trail in Acadia). No matter what your physical ability or endurance level, there's a hike out there for you.

Regardless of the style of the trail, you'll find that exploring on foot generally offers the best park experience. The relatively slow pace of walking brings you into closer contact with wildlife, and allows you to appreciate the way that different perspectives and the day's

Shenandoah National Park

BROOKIELAND/SHUTTERSTOCK ©

shifting light can alter the scenery. The satisfaction gained from completing a hike is also a worthy reward; it's one thing to admire the view over the rolling horizon from the road, it's another to ascend to a rocky summit high above the forest-covered slopes.

Each park chapter in this guide has its own Hiking or Activities section with descriptions of the parks' top hikes. We've done our best to cover a variety of trails, not just our favorites. Our goal with descriptions is less about navigation than it is about helping you choose which hikes to include in your trip. Detailed trail descriptions and maps are readily available at visitor centers in every park, and they will complement this guide well. Know your limitations, know the route you plan to take and pace yourself.

Backpacking

There are hundreds of amazing day hikes to choose from in the park system, but if you want the full experience, head out into the wilderness on an overnight trip. The claim that 99% of park visitors never make it into the backcountry may not be true everywhere, but you will unquestionably see far fewer people and witness exponentially more magic the further from a road you go. Backcountry campgrounds (such as Glade Creek in the New River Gorge) are also much more likely to have openings than park lodges and car campgrounds (which fill up months in advance), making accommodations less of a headache.

Even if you have no backpacking experience, don't consider it out of reach. Most national parks have at least a few backcountry campgrounds within a couple of hours' walk of a trailhead, making them excellent options for first-time backpackers. You will need gear, however: an appropriate backpack, tent, sleeping bag and pad, headlamp and food are all essential – as is a stove and fuel if you plan on hot meals. Facilities are minimal: some campgrounds

Cadillac Mountain

★ **Classic Day Hikes**

Cadillac Mountain (Acadia)

Old Rag Mountain (Shenandoah)

Long Point Trail (New River Gorge)

Flat Top Trail (Blue Ridge Parkway)

Appalachian Trail (section hike from Harpers Ferry)

have fire rings and a composting toilet. Water is rarely available, though there are often nearby streams for water, which you'll then have to filter and/or chemically treat.

Familiarize yourself with the park rules and backcountry ethics before heading out. You will need a permit in some places (Shenandoah) but not in others (New River Gorge); apply online well in advance through the National Park Service website for the particular park. Some park visitor centers have a backcountry desk, where you can apply for walk-in permits, get trail information, learn about wildlife (bear canisters or suspension bags for hanging food are generally required) and check conditions. Before hitting the trail, learn about low-impact camping principles at Leave No Trace (lnt.org).

Preparation & Safety

Walks can be as short or long as you like, but remember this when planning: be prepared. The wilderness may be unlike anything you have ever experienced, and designating certain parcels of land as 'national parks' has not tamed it.

The weather can be extraordinary in its unpredictability and sheer force. The summer sun is blazing hot, sudden thunderstorms can create flash floods, strong windstorms can rip or blow away a poorly staked tent and heavy snowfall can arrive with little warning at higher elevations in the winter.

No matter where you are, water should be the number one item on your packing checklist – always carry more than you think you'll need. If you're doing any backpacking, make sure you have a way to purify water, and check with rangers ahead of time about the availability of water along the trail.

Sunblock, a hat, ibuprofen and warm wind- and waterproof layers are all essentials when hiking in the mountains.

After the elements, getting lost is the next major concern. Most day hikes are well signed and visitors are numerous, but you should always take some sort of map. If you plan on going into the backcountry, definitely take a topographic (topo) map and a compass. You can pick up detailed maps in most visitor centers; National Geographic's *Trails Illustrated* series is generally excellent.

At lower elevations and in desert parks, always ask about ticks, poison oak, poison ivy and venomous snakes before heading out. Most day hikes are on well-maintained trails, but it's good to know what's out there.

Finally, all hikers, solo or not, should always remember the golden rule: let someone know where you are going and how long you plan to be gone.

Appalachian Trail

The storied Appalachian Trail (AT) is an irresistible draw for many hikers. Passing through 14 states over the course of 2190 miles, the trail has access points all over New England and the Mid-Atlantic.

Harpers Ferry is considered the mental halfway point of the trail (though the geographic midpoint is actually further north in Pennsylvania), and the national park site makes a fine gateway for a section hike before or after exploring the town's Civil War heritage. You can also visit the AT's unofficial HQ, the Appalachian Trail Conservancy (www.appalachian trail.org), which has exhibits on the famous route. It's also the best source of information on the AT.

Just over 100 miles of the AT passes through Shenandoah National Park. The trail traces the summits of the Blue Ridge Mountains, and Skyline Drive passes over the trail several dozen times. Virginia, incidentally, has over 500 miles of the trail, more than any other state.

An excellent time to hike here is in September or October, when traffic on the trails has dissipated somewhat and autumn leaves are at their finest. In October, however, snow should be expected.

Hikers on the AT sleep in backcountry shelters spaced 3 to 8 miles apart. Reservations are required unless you're traversing the entire trail as thru-hikers are exempt. If you're not thru-hiking, you'll need to make the necessary consecutive reservations well in advance, especially in the summer.

Rafting, Kayaking & Canoeing

Paddling by rafts, kayak or canoe gives you a unique perspective of places you often can't reach by other means. River-running opportunities abound, but trips in the New River Gorge area are legendary. Slicing from North Carolina into West Virginia, the New cuts a deep gorge known as the Grand Canyon of the East, producing frothy rapids in its wake.

Part of the same national park is the Gauley River, arguably among the world's finest white water. Revered for its ultra-steep and turbulent chutes, this venerable Appalachian river is a watery roller-coaster, dropping more than 668ft and churning up 100-plus rapids in a mere 25 miles. Six more rivers, all in the same neighborhood, offer training grounds for less-experienced river lovers.

Acadia is a kayaker's paradise. You can paddle through clear waters past rocky shores and forest-covered islands. There are also paddling opportunities on inland bodies of water, including Long Pond, Eagle Lake, Echo Lake and Jordan Pond. The national park runs half-day sea kayak tours as do several outfitters in Bar Harbor.

Boat Trips

Part of Acadia National Park resides on Isle au Haut, a rocky island reachable only by boat from Deer Isle. More remote than the parklands near Bar Harbor, it escapes the big summer crowds. If you're looking for an unspoiled, untouristed, unhyped outpost of Acadia... well, you've found it.

The island's main draw is the superb hiking along the coastal trails near Duck Harbor on the southwest side. Thick forests, wave-battered sea cliffs, trickling brooks and misty ponds are all part of its allure. On the island's northwest side lies the main settlement, also called Isle au Haut, with a tiny year-round population of about 70 residents, which triples during the warm summer months.

Another piece of Acadia lies along the Schoodic Peninsula, which can be reached by car – though it's much more enjoyable to take the ferry over from Bar Harbor. Once there, you'll have splendid views of Mt Desert Island and Cadillac Mountain. With a smooth surface and relatively gentle hills, the one-way loop road is also excellent for cycling (bikes are welcome aboard the ferries).

There are many boat tours available in the waters around Acadia. You might spot whales, porpoises, bald eagles, seals and more on narrated nature cruises. For something more

Racing the AT

Over the last 20 years, ultra-runners have set out to thru-hike the Appalachian Trail in record time. In 2011 Jennifer Pharr Davis paced the fastest known time by hiking it in 46 days and 11 hours, an average of 47 miles per day. Her record stood until 2015 when the well-known ultra-marathoner and author Scott Jurek, with film crews, corporate sponsorship and a fan following, managed to beat her record by three hours.

Several others chipped away at the record until 2018 when the Belgian Karel Sabbe utterly destroyed it. He completed the AT in 41 days and seven hours, beating the previous record by four days. He averaged nearly 53 miles per day and finished the last 100 miles by running for 40 hours straight.

vintage, you can board a four-masted schooner operated by Downeast Windjammer Cruises.

Rock Climbing

There's no sport quite like rock climbing. From a distance it appears to be a feat of sheer strength, but balance, creativity, technical know-how and a Zen-like sangfroid are all parts of the game.

Acadia has a handful of rewarding routes, and draws relatively few climbers to the area. A top destination is the Otter Cliffs, a 60ft wall that plunges into the sea, which can be reached by rappelling or top-roping down. You'll have to avoid going at high tide when rocks can get soaked, and the starting point for the climb at the cliff's base is underwater. Other good climbing routes are found on Precipice, South Bubble and the sea cliffs of Great Head. For bouldering, check out the oceanside area between Sand Beach and Otter Cliffs. Acadia Mountain Guides Climbing School (acadiamountainguides.com) leads trips (including winter mountaineering) and can get you outfitted.

With over 1400 established rock-climbing routes, the New River Gorge is a magnet for climbers. The hard sandstone rocks, ranging in height from 30ft to 120ft, are mostly for advanced climbers, with most routes falling in the 5.10 to 5.12 range.

Cycling & Mountain Biking

As a general rule, expect more options for two-wheeled fun just outside park boundaries. There are, however, some exceptions: in Acadia, you can go for leisurely spins along some 45 miles of carriage roads that crisscross the woodlands of Mt Desert Island. These smooth, car-free trails wind past valleys, rocky cliffs, lakes and ponds. And there's a bike-friendly shuttle bus that travels between Bar Harbor Village (where bikes are available for rent) and Eagle Lake.

Near the Cape Cod National Seashore, you can go for a spin on the Cape Cod Rail Trail, a glorious 22-mile paved greenway through forest, past cranberry bogs and along sandy ponds ideal for a dip. This rural route, formerly used as a railroad line, is one of the finest bike trails in all of New England. Bicycle rentals are available at the trailheads in Dennis and Wellfleet, and opposite the National Seashore's visitor center in Eastham. There's car parking at all four sites (free except for Nickerson).

In the New River Gorge area, you'll find four short trails ranging from 1 to 6 miles that are part of the Arrowhead Trails system. These take you on forested terrain, over rocky sections, up and down hills and through rhododendron tunnels.

Cycling within national parks on roadways can be a challenging and dangerous endeavor owing to heavy traffic and steep grades. Anyone who's been grazed by an RV mirror can attest to that. Note that mountain biking on trails is prohibited in most parks.

Winter Sports

Come winter, trails and roads in several parks get blanketed with snow and the crowds disappear. It's a magical time to visit, and those willing to step into skis or snowshoes and brave the elements will be rewarded.

The best park for both activities is Acadia. Those bike-friendly carriage roads, which carry cyclists in the summer, transform into groomed trails for cross-country skiing. Although much of the surrounding area shuts down in the winter, some places stay open including Cadillac Mountain Sports (www.cadillacsports.com) in Bar Harbor, where you can buy or rent gear.

Swimming

When the summer heat arrives, you can cool off in lakes, gurgling streams and waterfall-fed pools. As river rats the world over will attest, nothing beats dipping into a swimming hole and drip-drying on a rock in the sun. But be careful – every year swimmers drown in national park rivers. Always check with visitor centers about trouble spots and the safest places to swim. Unless you're certain about the currents, swim only where others are swimming.

Ocean beaches are well worth planning a trip around, and Cape Cod National Seashore and New York's Gateway National Recreation Area have lovely spots for frolicking in the waves. Surprisingly Acadia has one of Maine's loveliest sandy beaches, which is rather unimaginatively named Sand Beach.

Other top places to get wet are Overall Run Falls and Hazel Falls in Shenandoah, Glade Creek in New River Gorge, Echo Lake in Acadia, Deep Creek Lake and Swallow Falls State Park.

Fishing

For many, the idea of heading to the national parks without a fishing rod is ludicrous. You can find picturesque streams, lakes and rivers all across the region, particularly in the Blue Ridge Mountains, Shenandoah and the New River Gorge. The big draws are various species of trout (including brook trout and rainbow trout) as well as bass, bluegill, pick, whitefish and pike. You can also go ocean fishing for striped bass, bluefish and other species off the pristine beaches of Cape Cod National Seashore.

Wherever you fish, read up on local regulations. Fishing permits are always required, and those caught fishing without one will be fined. (Children under 16 are generally not required to have a license.) Some waters, including many streams and rivers, are catch-and-release only, and sometimes bait-fishing is prohibited. Certain native fish are often protected, and anglers in possession of these can be heavily fined. The best place to check regulations is online; check the Fish & Fishing section of the NPS (www.nps.gov/subjects/fishing) website.

Horseback Riding

Horseback riding is possible in many places, and outfitters within or immediately outside the parks can take you on memorable outings through forests, across creeks and up wooded slopes. Rides run $50 for an hour in Shenandoah to $100 for a half-day trip and $250 for an overnight camping ride in the New River Gorge area.

Gray seals, Cape Cod Seashore

Wildlife Watching

Beyond the big cities of the eastern seaboard, black bears still roam through primeval forests and the plaintive howl of a coyote pierces the night sky. Whether you're snapping photos of harbor seals on Cape Cod or stumbling upon white-tailed deer on a Shenandoah trail, the power of nature is all around you in the national parks of New England and the Mid-Atlantic.

White-Tailed Deer

One animal that most visitors see is the white-tailed deer, often spotted in Shenandoah and near the Blue Ridge Parkway. Tan or reddish brown in color (with a more grayish hue in winter), the white-tailed deer weighs between 100lb and 200lb (males can weigh up to 300lb). White-tailed deer are quite adept at avoiding prospective predators. They can run fast, reaching speeds up to 40mph, and can jump distances of up to 30ft.

Only the bucks (males) have antlers. These regrow each year, beginning in late spring and summer when they are covered in a protective hairlike membrane called 'velvet.' The antlers harden by fall, when bucks use them to fight and establish dominance over other males during the breeding season. They shed their antlers by winter (typically January or February) and shortly thereafter new growth begins anew.

Does (females) give birth about six months after mating, and have between one and three fawns. When a deer senses danger, it may stomp its hooves or snort to warn others. It may also raise its tail straight up, revealing its white underside. This instinct (called 'flagging') warns other deer of danger. It also helps the fawns follow their mother as they take flight.

Gray wolves and mountain lions used to prey on deer in Appalachia, though with the absence of these animals today, full-grown deer have few predators. Bobcats, coyotes and black bears will occasionally kill a fawn.

The best time to spot them is when they're foraging and feeding in the early morning and late afternoon. You can often find deer along Skyline Drive and at Big Meadows in Shenandoah. Deer sometimes wander across roads in forested areas, and there are numerous accidents owing to careless drivers. Be especially vigilant when driving between dusk and dawn, and don't speed.

Black Bears

The most famous resident of the northeastern parks is the American black bear. Up to 6ft long, and standing 3ft high at the shoulder, the American black bear is the symbol of the US Forest Service. Males typically weigh around 250lb (females are smaller and weigh around 100lb), though bears weighing up to 600lb have also been found. They may look like lumbering creatures when they walk, but black bears can run fast, reaching speeds of up to 30mph (faster than 100m world-record holder Usain Bolt). Black bears are omnivores and subsist on wild berries, acorns, grasses, tree buds, flowers and roots, with plant materials providing about 85% of their diet. The other 15% comes from insects, animal carrion and other sources of protein.

Black bears have better eyesight and hearing than humans, though their strongest sense is smell, which is about seven times keener than a dog's. They are most active in the early-morning and late-evening hours during the spring and summer. In the wild, bears live an average of 12 to 15 years.

Black bears are not true hibernators but do enter long periods of sleep. They may emerge from their winter dens periodically during unusually warm spells or if they are disturbed. Female bears sometimes have a surprise waiting for them when they awaken in the spring time, as their offspring are born during their winter sleep. Females typically give birth to one to four cubs every other year. The cubs arrive in January or February and remain close to the mother for about 18 months, or until she mates again. Mating typically takes place in July. Both male and female bears have more than one mate during the summer.

Estimates vary wildly for the population size of black bears in the Appalachia and New England region, with an estimated 1000 bears in Shenandoah alone. Black bears once roamed much of North America, but habitat loss has significantly diminished their range and numbers.

Black bears are usually not aggressive unless there are cubs nearby, but they will go after food or food odors. Make sure to store your food and trash properly, and hang food using a bear bag if you plan on backpacking.

Coyotes & Foxes

Coyotes have a wiry build with sandy-brown fur, bushy tails and upright ears. They resemble a medium-sized dog in size and rarely grow above 40lb. Intelligent and highly adaptable, coyotes are omnivores, eating birds, rabbits and other small prey as well as plants, fruits and carrion (typically 90% of a coyote's diet is meat). You may not see a coyote, but you can still look for its presence. Its footprints reveal large pads with four toes tipped

Black bear cubs, Shenandoah National Park

★ Best Wildlife Sightings

Black bears (Shenandoah)

Turkeys (Blue Ridge Parkway)

White-tailed deer (Skyline Drive)

Beavers (Acadia)

Otters (New River Gorge)

Harbor seals (Cape Cod National Seashore)

Black bear cubs, Shenandoah National Park

PHOTOS BY ANDY/SHUTTERSTOCK ©

with evident claws at the end of each appendage. If you camp in the park, you might also hear the soulful howl of a coyote – or perhaps more than one. In autumn and winter, this normally solitary creature gathers in small packs for more effective hunting.

Now present throughout Shenandoah and other parts of Appalachia, coyotes are relatively recent arrivals to the region. After wolves disappeared from the eastern US due to overhunting and habitat loss, the highly adaptable coyote filled the ecological niche of its bigger canine relatives.

True to name, red foxes have striking reddish-hued fur with white-tipped tails and darker colored lower legs. They weigh about half as much as a coyote. Their distinctive pelts made them an early target of fur traders. The most agile of hunters, red foxes quietly stalk before an explosive pounce onto their prey, which can include rabbits, mice, chipmunks, squirrels, birds and even large insects.

The gray fox is slightly smaller than the red fox with a rounder face and shorter snout. It has a coarser fur, with a more salt-and-pepper hue, and a black-tipped tail. They weigh about as much as a sturdy house cat, about 12lb on average. They have semi-retractable claws, which give them the unique ability to climb trees and means their footprints may resemble a cat's (without the appearance of claws).

Beavers

Described by scientists as a 'keystone' species, beavers are vital, and without them an ecosystem can collapse. They are prolific builders, gnawing through trees and branches, which they carry between their teeth. Combining the timber with mud and small stones, beavers build dams and lodges – feats of engineering that have a profound effect on the landscape.

By blocking streams, they flood the surrounding forest, which creates an ideal environment to raise their young; the lodges they build are only accessible by an underwater entrance, a strong deterrent to predators. The newly formed ponds benefit plant and animal life, with some tree species (like the willow) flourishing from the abundant water source.

Beavers can grow 2ft long and typically weigh between 30lb and 60lb. They are excellent swimmers and can see well underwater, though they have relatively poor eyesight on land. They mate for life and each lodge contains a pair of adults and their offspring (kits). Before winter, beavers store tree bark and roots to get them through when other food sources are scarce. At other times of year, they eat aquatic plants as well as forest fruits and berries.

Flying Squirrels

The flying squirrel has big eyes, a pink nose, long whiskers and a small furry body, which can glide silently through the air as the animal leaps from treetop to treetop. Although not actually capable of flight, these small rodents have a patagium – a furry, parachute-like membrane stretching from the front paws to the hind legs. This allows them to take dramatic leaps through the branches, soaring across distances of more than 200ft. There are two species of the animal in Appalachia: the southern flying squirrel and the northern flying squirrel. The southern is the smaller, stretching about 9in from nose to tail and often weighing just 2oz or 3oz (about as much as a deck of playing cards). The southern is also the more common. The northern flying squirrel is about 30% larger, and lives only at higher elevations (above 4500ft) in conifer forests. Owing to habitat loss, the northern flying squirrel is now listed as endangered. Both squirrels are nocturnal, and sightings are rare.

Bobcats

The bobcat is likely the only wild feline living in these eastern national parks. True to name, bobcats have short, stumpy tails and can weigh up to 70lb. These solitary creatures, with their spotted fur and tufted ears, are quite striking, though rarely spotted owing to their nocturnal habits. There are occasional reports of cougar sightings in the Appalachia region, but no concrete evidence of their presence has been found in more than three decades.

Pygmy Shrews

A fine counterpoint to the mighty black bear is the pygmy shrew, a rare and diminutive creature so tiny that it weighs less than a penny. It's one of 11 species of mole or shrew found in the Appalachia region, and isn't often spotted since it spends most of its time underground, burrowing in search of tasty insects.

Marine Mammals

Several species of whale pass through the waters off New England's coastline. These include the massive finback whale, which can grow up to 80ft long, as well as humpback and minke whales. The critically endangered North Atlantic right whale is extremely rare, with only about 300 left in the world.

In Acadia, you may occasionally spot harbor seals. These doe-eyed creatures are relatively small (5ft long, up to 250lb) and sometimes pop up on rocky shores (usually in isolated human-free environments). In spring, harbor seals give birth to their offspring. Pups are left alone on the coastline (for upward of 24 hours) and might appear to be abandoned, but in fact their mothers are usually feeding nearby. It is illegal to handle or disturb these animals.

Bigger in size than harbor seals, gray seals can grow up to 10ft long and weigh upwards of 800lb. They too are making a comeback in New England, with a population size of around 400,000 that move up and down the Atlantic coast between Canada and North Carolina. Until 1972 there was a bounty on seals, as fishermen believed the seals would decimate valuable cod-fishing grounds, though there is little evidence that seals compete with fishers. Hunters slaughtered the animals in huge numbers.

You can see both harbor and gray seals in Cape Cod throughout the year. One of the best times to see them, though, is after the start of breeding season (which runs from September through March) when large numbers of seals arrive.

Sharks

The most powerful apex predator off the coast of New England is the great white shark. Once an extreme rarity in these parts of the country, great whites are now spotted regularly off the coast of Cape Cod. Their increasing prevalence is directly linked to the resurgence of their favorite prey, the seal, as well as warming coastal waters as a result of climate change. Though feared and reviled, the great white plays a critical role in maintaining a healthy marine ecosystem.

Warmer weather parallels the busiest season of great whites, with sightings off the coast of New York and New England peaking from July to October. A few tips for shark safety include staying close to the shore when venturing out, avoiding swimming where seals are present, and not isolating yourself (whether swimming, paddling, kayaking or surfing).

Notify a lifeguard if you do spot a shark, as the water will then be closed to recreational activities until the danger has passed. If you're particularly keen on keeping up-to-date with these marine carnivores, download the Sharktivity app, which allows researchers and app users alike to post shark sightings in order to reduce dangerous encounters and promote safety.

Attacks are fairly rare, however. Since 2012, there have been four unprovoked attacks by great whites, one of them fatal.

Birds

Birding is the most popular wildlife-watching activity in the US, and little wonder – you'll find an astonishing array of migratory songbirds and shorebirds, and more than 600 bird species nest here or migrate through the region.

Birds of Prey

Birds of prey – including eagles, falcons, hawks, owls and harriers – are common in the parks, with several dozen species present.

The bald eagle was adopted as the nation's symbol in 1782. It's the only eagle unique to North America, and perhaps half a million once ruled the continent's skies. By 1963 habitat destruction and, in particular, poisoning from DDT had caused the population to plummet to 487 breeding pairs in the lower 48 states. By 2007, however, bald eagles had recovered so well, increasing to almost 9800 breeding pairs across the continent, that they were removed from the endangered species list. Today they are found in every state apart from Hawaii, with an estimated 300,000 in the US.

Peregrine falcons also nest in Maine, and, like bald eagles, have made a remarkable comeback since the 1970s. The world's fastest animal, peregrine falcons can reach speeds of up to 180mph when diving for prey from lofty heights. Osprey, which nest and hunt around rivers and lakes, are another commonly spotted raptor.

Aquatic Birds

Many avian species flourish in the estuaries, mudflats and salt marshes, where wading birds such as the great blue heron, snowy egret and glossy ibis can be spotted.

Lakes and ponds provide key habitats for some species, including the iconic common loon in the northeast. These black-and-white plumed birds, with their distinctive red eyes, are known for their haunting calls. Though their numbers reached record lows by the 1970s, their population has stabilized in recent years.

Amphibians & Reptiles

Frogs, toads and salamanders thrive in and around streams, rivers and lakes in several of the parks. With 24 species of salamanders, southern Appalachia is often deemed the salamander capital of the world.

Love 'em or hate 'em, snakes are here to stay in most of the parks – but snakebites are rare. Along with over a dozen harmless species, the region has timber rattlesnakes and copperheads: two venomous species present in many places (Acadia has no venomous snakes), but they are generally not aggressive and would rather flee than bite.

Creek, Blue Ridge Mountains

Conservation

Protecting the region's wild spaces has been a challenge since the creation of Acadia – the first national park east of the Mississippi – in 1919. The parks now safeguard some of the greatest natural treasures on the planet. But they face new, often concurrent, threats. Climate change, invasive species and pollution all jeopardize the national parks today.

Climate Change

Major voices within the National Parks Service, in agreement with scores of eminent scientists and climatologists, worry that climate change poses a significant threat to the health of the network's diverse ecosystems. Although park biologists are only just beginning to understand the impact of climate change, nearly all agree that it's taking a toll.

Climate change has led to the creation of more powerful storms and record-shattering rainfalls. Warmer temperatures are also affecting a wide variety of plant and animal life. Among other species, brook trout are disappearing from Shenandoah and the southern Appalachians owing to rising water temperatures. Scientists predict 97% of brook trout habitat could disappear.

Abandoned coal tower, New River Gorge National Park

Increased sea levels and higher storm surges are impacting Cape Cod National Sea-shore and other coastal areas. Sea levels on the Cape have risen 11in since 1922, leading to beach erosion, destruction of marshes and damage to vital infrastructure.

Invasive Species

Invasive species pose a severe threat to the national parks. In the southern Appalachians, a non-native insect called the hemlock woolly adelgid is decimating eastern hemlock forests. In Shenandoah, where the insect has been present since 1980, nearly 95% of the hemlocks have perished.

The seemingly innocuous common reed is a significant threat to North America's wetlands, including the Cape Cod National Seashore. The fast-growing perennial grass originally from Eurasia can spread at a rate of 16ft per year, outcompeting – and ultimately wiping out – other vegetation.

Acadia faces a whole range of invasive plants and animals, including Asian shore crabs that threaten intertidal species, European fire ants that are outcompeting native ant spe-cies and Asian long-horned beetles that tunnel through many species of deciduous trees.

Of course, we can hardly remove ourselves from the list of invasive species. Each year millions of visitors travel to and through the parks. Traffic, roads, encroaching development and the simple fact of human presence in sensitive wildlife areas all have an effect on park ecosystems.

Pollution

Aside from the impact visitors make on the parks, humans are putting immense pressure on many parks in New England and the mid-Atlantic owing to carbon emissions from big cities, heavy industry and the abundance of cars and trucks. Shenandoah is sometimes rated as the second most polluted park in the country thanks to nearby coal- and oil-burning power plants.

The waters of Cape Cod National Seashore and New York Harbor have been polluted by run-off from fertilizers, garden chemicals, oil and gas leaks from automobiles, septic systems and other contaminants. This can destroy animal habitats and lead to fish kills.

Meanwhile, the New River Gorge has been deeply impacted by deep mining for coal along with gas and oil operations. There are over 100 abandoned mine sites that post environmental hazards to the region. Exacerbating the environmental problems are the poor air quality and waste from illegal dumps.

Sustainable Visitation

As magnificent as they are, national park sites receive only a tiny percentage of the US national budget, and have often struggled to get adequate funding. The $9.5-billion Great American Outdoors Act, passed in 2020, will address long-deferred maintenance – but much more is needed to ensure the viability of the parks in the decades ahead.

Visitors can make a positive impact by traveling sustainably and getting involved with park associations. Whenever you can, ride park shuttles or hop on a bike instead of driving your car. Skip high-impact park activities such as helicopter flights over New York Harbor or big bus tours around the National Mall. Prevent erosion by always staying on trails. If you're backpacking, use biodegradable soaps (or skip them altogether) and follow the principles of Leave No Trace (lnt.org).

Nearly every site run by the National Park Service has an associated foundation or other nonprofit that supports its parent park. These organizations, which include Friends of Acadia (www.friendsofacadia.org), Shenandoah National Park Trust (www.snptrust.org) and Friends of the Cape Cod National Seashore (www.fccns.org), conduct everything from trail maintenance and coastal cleanups to habitat restoration. Members can volunteer or donate to programs that are critical to the parks' well-being.

Meanwhile, the National Parks Conservation Association (www.npca.org) covers all of the parks. Since 1919 this nonprofit organization has been protecting and preserving America's national parks through research, advocacy and education.

Landscapes & Geology

The clashing of supersized continents, glacial ice sheets and primordial river systems have all played prominent roles in shaping this geologically diverse region. Nature appears in ways big (age-old Appalachian peaks) and small (low-lying kettle ponds on the shores of Cape Cod), and learning the story behind its landscapes can add a new level of depth to your travels here.

Tectonic Forces

Some 500 million years ago, before craggy peaks studded the horizon, this area was little more than a shallow marine region along the continental edge. Fossilized remains of burrows and the shells of ancient sea creatures can be found on bedding surfaces of rocks in some areas. Ancient fossils have also been found including trilobites (an extinct marine arthropod) and the teeth of 500-million-year-old conodonts (akin to small eels). Some rock formations are even older, dating back more than a billion years, created by the melding of marine deposits and igneous rock in a primordial ocean.

Things started to get interesting around 300 million years ago when two massive landmasses collided. Present-day North America, part of the larger landmass of Laurasia (which also included Eurasia), crashed into Gondwana (comprising present-day Africa and

South America), becoming part of the single supercontinent of Pangaea. The collision of tectonic plates over millions of years placed tremendous pressure and heat, and caused horizontal layers of rock to be thrust upward, thus creating the massive Central Pangaean mountain chain – of which the Appalachian (and Smokies) were a part.

Around 200 million years ago, the supercontinent began to break apart, with massive landmasses peeling off, and the North American and African tectonic plates slowly moved to their current position. After their formation, the Appalachian Mountains were much higher than they are today. Some geologists believe these mountains were once as high as, or even higher than, the Himalayas. The forces of erosion, caused by wind, water and ice, wore down these soaring peaks over millions of years, with vast quantities of sediment carried toward the Atlantic Ocean and the Gulf of Mexico – even forming some of the beaches on America's southern shores. The erosion process continues even today at the rate of around 2in every 1000 years.

The Ice Age

Fast forward through time to around two million years ago, when the earth entered a cold spell (aka the Pleistocene Epoch) and plunging temperatures initiated the Great Ice Age. Glacial ice marched across the continent (and across huge swaths of the globe), melted, then advanced once again over at least a dozen different periods. As glaciers flowed over the landscape, they eroded mountains, carved deep valleys and even altered the geography of the Ohio River and other waterways.

The final episode happened around 20,000 years ago during the so-called Wisconsin Glaciation. That's when the ice sheets reached their maximum extent, growing up to 1 mile thick and stretching across all of present-day New England and New York as well as parts of New Jersey, Pennsylvania and the Upper Midwest. When they retreated, they transformed the landscape, sometimes strewing boulders (aka glacial erratics) and other debris miles away from their origin.

Acadia's Mt Desert Island was sheared from the mainland by the action of glaciers. Much of Cape Cod was formed by glaciers, with deposits some 200ft to 600ft accumulating on the cape. You'll even find some massive chunks of other mountains like Doane Rock, a 45ft behemoth (one-third of which lies below ground) and the largest exposed boulder found on Cape Cod. One of Acadia's most photographed formations is Bubble Rock, a near spherical glacial erratic that sits at the top of South Bubble Mountain.

Forests of Appalachian Mountains

During the ice age, the Appalachian Mountains became a refuge for many species of plants and animals that retreated south from the colder northern climes. This contributed to the great diversity of the region's forests: there are more tree species here than in all of Europe. Although glaciers weren't present in southern Appalachia, the ice age also left its mark in other ways. As the mountains froze and thawed, rocks of all sizes sheered off and tumbled down the slopes and into the valleys below, creating curious boulder fields amid the forests that stand today.

The forests are home to over 150 native tree species and more than 1800 types of vascular plants. Much of this diversity is due to the wide variations of elevation (from 875ft to above 6600ft) and geography, with a mix of both southern and northern species. Abundant rainfall and high humidity in the warmer months also provides ideal growing conditions.

New River Gorge National Park

MALACHI JACOBS/SHUTTERSTOCK ©

★ **Rock Star Vistas**

Cadillac Mountain (Acadia)

The Point Overlook (Shenandoah)

Herring Cove Beach (Cape Cod National Seashore)

Thunder Hill Overlook (Blue Ridge Parkway)

Beauty Mountain (New River Gorge)

Pine & Oak Forests

In the mountains up to about 4500ft, where the slopes are dry and exposed, you can expect to find forests dominated by pine and oak trees. Thickets of mountain laurel and stands of rhododendron grow well here, as do flowering dogwood trees, galax, yellow poplars and hickory. Of the various species of oak and pine, the most commonly found trees are scarlet oak, chestnut oak, black oak, Table Mountain pine, Virginia pine and pitch pine. Forest fires are not uncommon in these habitats and can be necessary for some species' reproduction and forest regeneration.

Cove Forests

In Appalachian parlance, coves are sheltered valleys with deep, fertile soils. These are some of the most botanically diverse forests, which grow on forested slopes, and they also support a rich variety of animal life. You'll find tulip tree, yellow buckeye, sugar maple, black cherry, magnolia, yellow birch and Carolina silverbell among dozens of other species. Wildflowers are also profuse in these forests, and autumn colors are dazzling.

Spruce & Fir Forest

In the southern Blue Ridge Mountains, you'll find these iconic evergreen forests. Also called boreal or Canadian zone forests, the spruce-fir forests grow at elevations above 4500ft and share characteristics of habitats in eastern Canada. They are a legacy of the ice age, when northern plants migrated south to escape the continental glaciers. When the weather warmed, these northern species remained, continuing to thrive on the cool mountain summits. Today two coniferous species rule the ridges: Fraser firs and red spruce. Unfortunately, these forests are being decimated by a non-native insect, with the balsam woolly adelgid wiping out the Fraser fir population.

Appalachian Balds

In some places at high elevations, there are patches of land entirely devoid of trees. These include grassy balds, which are not unlike highland meadows (more commonly observed in lowland prairies), and heath balds, covered in thickets of mountain laurel and rhododendrons. How these unique Appalachian land features formed remains something of a mystery. Grassy balds were used by early settlers to graze their livestock, though scientists have determined through soil samples that these tree-free areas existed even before the sheep and cattle arrived. Another theory is that megafauna – herbivorous mastodons and woolly mammoths – grazed here some 10,000 years ago.

The American Chestnut

American chestnuts once made up about one-third of the trees in the Appalachians. In springtime their blossoms were so thick that the mountains appeared as if they were covered in snow. Then in the first half of the 20th century, a fungus from Asia swept across the country, killing every American chestnut in its path. By 1950 an estimated four billion trees had died, and the American chestnut forest had been wiped forever from the planet. Botanists describe the chestnut blight as the largest ecological catastrophe in North America during the 20th century.

American chestnuts were once lords of the forest, with their treetops stretching up to 120ft high. You can still see their stumps in some parks, some of which even sprout. These young saplings don't reach very high before they too are felled by the blight, which continues to live deep in the trees' roots.

Some naturalists, however, haven't given up hope that the chestnut may some day

What's in a name?

If ever there were a contest for the most poorly chosen name, the New River would surely win the prize. There's no consensus among geologists, but some scientists believe this river system is some 300 million years old, making it one of the oldest waterways on the planet. Flowing through the Appalachians, the New may be older than the mountains themselves, having risen with them as they formed. The name's origin is shrouded in mystery, though one theory places the blame on two 17th-century explorers. On their journey across Appalachia, Thomas Batts and Robert Fallam came across a river that they didn't recognize, and simply labeled it as 'new' on their maps. Subsequent mapmakers simply repeated the error and the name stuck.

make a comeback. A group of researchers from West Virginia University have discovered a virus that attacks the blight-causing fungus. If they can replicate the virus and move it from tree to tree, the American chestnut may be able to grow and thrive once again. Yet another group is cross-breeding American chestnuts with blight-resistant Chinese chestnuts, in the hope of creating a new strain of tree that can someday return to the American forests.

The Eastern Seaboard

Beaches, islands, bays, estuaries, tidal marshes and rocky shorelines all provide unique habitats for the flora and fauna of New England and the Mid-Atlantic. In contrast to the Paleozoic-era mountainous interior, much of this coastal region has evolved in more recent times.

Cape Cod National Seashore

Cape Cod is a youngster in geologic terms, having only appeared since the retreat of glaciers less than 20,000 years ago. Since that time, over 800 plant species have flourished, many of which have adapted to the unique coastal environment, and grow amid the diverse ecosystems on the Cape. Intertidal zones, salt marshes, dunes and forests all have different types of plant communities. Humans have also shaped the landscape. The clearing of land by 17th-century colonists, as well as fires, led to a dramatic growth of heathlands and grasslands, which outcompeted other endemic floral species. Without these disturbances, much of the cape would be covered in forests.

Dunes also play a role in the island's ecology. They comprise one-third of the Cape's land surface. Plants that grow on the dunes have adapted to the harsh environment of wind, aridity and salt, and protect the dunes and the surrounding land by stabilizing the shore and preventing erosion. Near the shore, salt marshes filter out nutrients and serve as a vital habitat for birds, fish and crustaceans.

Inland, small bodies of freshwater provide further evidence of the Cape's glacial past. Kettles, or depressions, were formed by melting ice chunks that then filled with groundwater and precipitation. These kettle ponds are sprinkled across much of the Cape and provide habitats for plant and animal life, including a dozen species of amphibians as well as reptiles. Freshwater ponds and grasslands are also essential resources for the abundant migratory and resident birdlife – with some 370 bird species present during the year.

Acadia National Park

Further north of Cape Cod along the central coast of Maine, Acadia has an unusual combination of features not found in other parts of New England. You'll find the tallest mountains on the eastern seaboard, subalpine rocky summits, as well as woodlands, wetlands, lakes and streams. Acadia lies in a transition area between two different zones. Eastern deciduous forests, commonly found further south, are dominated by leaf-losing trees such as maples, oaks and beeches. Northern boreal forests, which stretch up to the edge of the Arctic, feature spruce, fir, hemlock, juniper and other evergreens (trees and shrubs that keep their green needle-like leaves year-round), as well as birches. Millions of migratory birds pass over each year as Acadia is located on the Atlantic Flyway.

Gateway National Recreation Area

Despite its location near one of the most heavily populated areas in America, the protected areas of New York Harbor support a surprising variety of plant and animal life. One of the most surprising species is the eastern prickly pear cactus, which can be found in sandy soil in sunny areas through the Gateway National Recreation Area. The only cactus native to the northeast, the eastern prickly pear is most striking in May and June when it produces yellow, waxy flowers sometimes with a red or orange center. These eventually die away and are replaced by red, edible fruits.

Apart from beaches and sand dunes, you'll find grasslands, forests, salt marshes and woodlands. These habitats are vital during the spring and fall migration when over 330 bird species pass through along the Atlantic Flyway.

Behind The Scenes

Acknowledgements

Climate map data adapted from Peel MC, Finlayson BL & McMahon TA (2007) 'Updated World Map of the Köppen-Geiger Climate Classification', *Hydrology and Earth System Sciences*, 11, pp1633–44.

Cover photograph: Blue Ridge Mountains from Blackrock Summit, Shenandoah National Park, Jon Bilous/Shutterstock©

Send Us Your Feedback

We love to hear from travelers – your comments keep us on our toes and help make our books better. Our well-traveled team reads every word on what you loved or loathed about this book. Although we cannot reply individually to postal submissions, we always guarantee that your feedback goes straight to the appropriate authors, in time for the next edition. Each person who sends us information is thanked in the next edition.

Visit lonelyplanet.com/contact to submit your updates and suggestions or to ask for help. Our award-winning website also features inspirational travel stories, news and discussions.

Note: We may edit, reproduce and incorporate your comments in Lonely Planet products such as guidebooks, websites and digital products, so let us know if you don't want your comments reproduced or your name acknowledged. For a copy of our privacy policy visit lonelyplanet.com/legal.

This Book

This 1st edition of Lonely Planet's *New England & the Mid-Atlantic's National Parks* was researched and written by Regis St Louis, Amy Balfour, Robert Balkovich, Virginia Maxwell and Karla Zimmerman.

This guidebook was produced by the following:

Commissioning Editor Angela Tinson
Design Development Katherine Marsh
Cartographic Series Designer Wayne Murphy
Product Editor Kate James
Senior Cartographer Anthony Phelan
Book Designer Norma Brewer
Assisting Editors Janet Austin, Imogen Bannister, Melanie Dankel, Gabrielle Innes
Production Development Liz Heynes, Dianne Schallmeiner, John Taufa, Juan Winata
Cover Researcher Gwen Cotter
Thanks to Sonia Kapoor

Index

A

Acadia National Park 4, 24-5, 38-49, 132, **39**
accommodations 15
  Acadia National Park 42
  New River Gorge National Park 90
  Shenandoah National Park 64
activities 16-18, 34-5, 114-19, *see also individual activities*
African American Civil War Memorial 86
African Burial Ground National Monument 57
animals 120-4
Antietam National Battlefield 72
Appalachian Trail 7, 92-7, 116-17, 118
Appomattox Court House National Park 77
art galleries, *see* museums & galleries

B

Bar Harbor 46
Bass Harbor Head Lighthouse 46
beaches
  Coast Guard Beach 51
  Gateway National Recreation Area 56
  Head of the Meadow Beach 54
  Herring Cove Beach 51
  Marconi Beach 50
  Nauset Light Beach 51
  Race Point beach 54
  Sand Beach 45

beavers 122
Bedford 102
Beehive Loop 48-9
Berkeley Springs 94
bicycle travel, *see* cycling
birds 124
Blackwater Falls State Park 96
boat trips 117-18
bobcats 123
books 19
budget 15

C

Cadillac Mountain Summit Loop 39, 46
camping 15
canoeing 117
Cape Cod National Seashore 12, 50-5, 131-2
children, travel with 32-3
cinema 19
Civil War 110-11
Civil War sites 8, 78-81
  Antietam National Battlefield 72
  Appomattox Court House 77
  Cold Harbor Battlefield 76
  Contrabands & Freedmen Cemetery Memorial 79
  Fort Warren 79
  Fredericksburg & Spotsylvania National Military Park 74
  Gettysburg National Military Park 80
  Harriet Tubman Underground Railroad National Historic Park 78
  Manassas National Battlefield (Bull Run) 74
  Monocacy National Battlefield 78
  Petersburg National Battlefield Park 77

  Stonewall Jackson Shrine 74, 76
Civilian Conservation Corps (CCC) 112
climate 14, 16-18
climate change 106-7, 125
climbing 89, 118
clothing 22-3
Cold Harbor Battlefield 76
conservation 125-7
Constitution Gardens 84
costs 15
coyotes 121-2
cycling 118
  Acadia National Park 39
  Cape Cod National Seashore 55
  New River Gorge National Park 90
  Shenandoah National Park 63

D

dangers, *see* safety
Deep Creek Lake 94, 96
deer 120-1
Dinosaur Land 66
driving tours
  Acadia National Park 44-7, **45**
  Across the Appalachian Trail 92-7, **93**
  Blue Ridge Parkway 98-103, **99**
  Civil War Tour 72-7, **73**
  Skyline Drive 66-71, **67**

E

Ellis Island 58
emergencies 21, 23
environmental issues 106-7, 125-7
equipment 22-3
events 16-18

000 Map pages